YOU CAN'T ASK THAT!

50 TABOO QUESTIONS ABOUT THE BIBLE, JESUS, AND CHRISTIANITY

EDITED BY CHRISTIAN PIATT

chalice
press

Saint Louis, Missouri

An imprint of Christian Board of Publication

ChalicePress.com

Print 9780827244313

EPUB 9780827244320

EPDF 9780827244337

Printed in the United States of America

CONTENTS

FOREWORD

A few years ago, I traveled to Jordan with Christian Piatt and a group of faith writers and church leaders. We stood together in the rubble of ancient ruins, explored biblical landmarks, and visited places of spiritual significance. It was the trip of a lifetime, but of all the incredible things we saw and did, it's the least remarkable place that I think of most often.

At our first stop, the tour bus pulled off the highway into a small gravel lot. Traffic sped past us on one side, filling our lungs with dust and exhaust fumes, and on the other side, a polluted stream trickled along. There was garbage and graffiti everywhere, and on the far side of the creek, an odd pair of pants had been perfectly laid out to dry in the dirt. We took it all in while our tour guide gathered us close enough to be heard over the road noise and explained that we were standing where Jacob wrestled an angel by a river, as told in Genesis. It happened right there. Next to a filthy freeway underpass… where someone lost their pants.

I looked to Christian, my fellow skeptic, who looked back at me with a proper side-eye, like, *"Really?"*

I had so many questions.

At every stop throughout the trip, our tour guide spoke about theology, archeology, geography, and history with great authority, as if there was no doubt he spoke truth. Most of the people in the group embraced his teaching with gusto and then confidently passed the information along to their churches, readers, and families as stated fact. It was amazing to see how quickly a trash-strewn patch of gravel by the side of the road became the undisputed wrestling mat of Jacob and an angel.

Each night, I met Christian and a few of our doubt-filled cohorts at the hotel bar, where we talked too loud, drank too much, and asked all of the big, scary questions the day's travel had inspired. Questions like, "If I believe Jacob *literally* wrestled an angel at a truck stop in Jordan, do I have to take everything in the Bible literally?" and, "What if I don't believe the Bible is literal *at all*?"

In my own journey, I've found few things as encouraging as other people's questions. It's just nice to know I'm not the only person with questions about Jesus, and sex, and heaven, and all of those weird Bible stories full of incest and foreskins and stuff. As my faith has evolved and my questions have grown both bigger and more nuanced, I've had few friends who are as eager to explore complicated questions as Christian Piatt.

You Can't Ask That is a perfect example of Christian's ability to challenge the mysteries of faith without settling for easy answers. He did the hard part by posing our messiest questions to a variety of wise, experienced leaders, and gathering their thoughtful responses together in one place. Reading this book reminded me of the late night, whiskey-driven chats we shared in Jordan. During that trip, I found the most compelling questions, honest conversations, and informative responses happened at the hotel bar with Christian and our circle of friends.

In *You Can't Ask That* I think you'll find that Christian Piatt has dared to ask and seek answers to some of your own big, scary, taboo questions. I hope these pages and the wealth of insight and resources they contain will help you to feel seen and understood, and even more, that they may help you see and understand others. But if any of the questions or answers start to make you squirm, just think of this book as a chic hotel bar or a toasty firepit where you're chatting with a circle of friends.

Among friends there are no taboos.

— Jamie Wright
Author of *The Very Worst Missionary:*
A Memoir or Whatever

INTRODUCTION

But Why?

There's a three-letter word that can cause entire institutions to shiver to their collective foundations. In systems where uniformity and compliance are necessary for survival, this tiny word can seem to chip away at the cornerstone, propping the whole thing up.

And yet it's one of the first words every one of us learns as toddlers.

Anyone who has been around children for long knows how tedious the word can be, but for the kid, it serves as a key that helps open the door to a world of understanding.

WHY?

As a student in parochial school, I was taught the value of debate, critical thought, and rhetoric. But then when I got to church, I was expected to listen, accept, and not challenge what I was taught.

In fact, when I asked one too many questions, they threw me out. Even chucked a Bible at my head during youth group in case I wasn't getting the message.

My questions posed a threat.

Ideally, though, questions present an invitation into shared exploration, discussion, and growth. All that is required for us to make this shift is to let go of the need to be *right* for the sake of the possibility to be *changed.*

The 50 questions in this book were pulled from the Banned Questions series. I've presented multiple responses to each question in this volume because there isn't necessarily one "right answer." Instead, the questions themselves are the most important thing, followed by what new paths those questions lead us along.

What will we find? How might we change? The only way to know is to ask the hard questions and see where we end up.

Why not?

— *Christian Piatt*

1

Can I be a Christian if I don't believe the Bible is perfect, handed down directly from God to humanity without error?

....

Craig Detweiler

Absolutely. Scientific principles have only been applied to the Bible for a couple hundred years. An earlier era understood divine inspiration as a different kind of truth. Shoehorning the Bible into scientific standards may actually reduce the profound gifts that the Bible provides. Shakespeare is not intended to be crammed into a test tube. Surely the Bible operates on an entirely different plane and claim to authority.

For example, we know that love is a powerful, elusive, but tangible reality. Artists and musicians have given us countless ways to describe such a profound truth. Drugs have enhanced the physical side of sexual performance. Yet medical breakthroughs cannot make us more loving. Becoming more loving is a lifelong quest, rooted in prayer, perseverance, and careful attention to others.

Following Jesus (the core Christian route) involves so much more than the minutiae of the Bible. We may memorize countless verses, but we are still called to put them into practice. Jesus seemed so interested in how our convictions turned into tangible differences for our communities. He gave little time or attention to those who tried to trap him into semantic arguments about obscure interpretations of the Torah. The Bible speaks into our hearts and minds with both veracity and variety. It is meant to woo, to persuade, to challenge, not by nailing down the details but pushing us toward applying timeless truths for today.

....

Jason Boyett

Of course. Belief in the inerrancy of scripture—inerrancy is the theological word for the idea that the Bible is without error—is not a requirement for salvation. Let me be clear: A Christian is not someone who believes in the perfection of scripture. A Christian is someone who follows Jesus Christ.

Remember, the earliest Christians didn't even have the Bible as we know it. They had the Law and the Prophets on ancient scrolls. Certain churches had letters written by Paul. A few may have had the gospel accounts to read (and many certainly had other noncanonical gospels available, such as the gospel of Thomas). But they most likely wouldn't have made a big deal about whether or not these texts were free from chronological or scientific errors because they just didn't think that way.

The idea that the Bible's authority is tied to its lack of mistakes is an Enlightenment idea. In the grand arc of history, that's a pretty recent concept.

That's not to say the Bible isn't inspired or authoritative. It certainly is inspired in that it tells us the story of Jesus, from Genesis to Revelation. It is authoritative in that it is God's primary means of communicating with us. But the Bible is not part of the Trinity; to exalt it above the Christ whose story it tells, and whose salvation it reveals, is a bad idea.

· ·
José F. Morales Jr.

A. Nowhere in the Bible does it say that one must believe in the Bible (let alone believe it's perfect) to be saved. Moreover, the Bible doesn't claim authority for itself within its pages. That's why I contend with my fellow Christians who say that one must believe in the "authority of the Bible." For me, the awesomeness of the Bible is that it points beyond itself.

And to what does it point?

First, the Bible points to the authority of God—not of the Bible! God is supreme above all, creator and sustainer of all life—life now and beyond the grave. I always say that the most important words in scripture are the first four: "In the beginning, God . . ."

Second, the Bible points to the good news of salvation. Now, salvation is defined in many different ways throughout scripture. So we should become familiar with the broad stroke with which the Bible paints salvation: God saves in creation, in gathering a community, in political liberation, in acquiring wisdom, in healing, and in the washing away of sin. In his book *Salvation*, Joel Green summarizes it best: Salvation is "God drawing near"—drawing near in creation, in the Temple, in Christ.

And we draw near to the Bible, the written word, because in doing so, the Living Word, whom Christians know as Jesus Christ, draws near to us (see Lk. 24:13–32). "They said to each other, 'Were not our hearts burning within us while he [Jesus] was talking to us on the road, while he was opening the scriptures to us?'" (Lk. 24:32).

God indeed has drawn near to save us—believe it!

· ·
Nadia Bolz-Weber

A. A World Religions professor of mine in seminary told a story about New Testament scholar John Dominic Crossan being asked what it takes to be a Christian. His answer? "If you're dipped, you're in." What

Crossan was saying is that your baptism makes you Christian. And when we are baptized, it is in the name of the Father, and of the Son, and of the Holy Spirit.

Notice that we are not baptized in the name of the Bible. Why is this? Because the Bible is not the fourth person of the Trinity, even though it is often treated as such.

Again, this is where Lutherans get in trouble with some of our other Christian brothers and sisters. We believe that God claims us and names us as God's own in the waters of baptism. The action is from God toward us, not from us toward God.

For a really great treatment on the difference between viewing the Bible as Divine Reference Manual and viewing the Bible as Living Word, see *Making Sense of Scripture* by David J. Lose.

. . . .

Christian Piatt

A. There are two things to consider when dealing with this question: church history and human nature. One of the biggest reasons that Martin Luther resisted the authority of the Catholic Church the way he did, ultimately sparking the Protestant Reformation, was because he believed that people should not be beholden to the church in claiming what they believe about God.

So at the foundation of every non-Catholic Christian church is this value of the individual freedom of belief, at least in theory. But in reality, we humans aren't big fans of letting go of control, and church is certainly no exception. Although Baptists, Methodists, Lutherans, and all other Protestants supposedly have the liberty to interpret scripture without organized religion interceding and telling them what to think, we find plenty of examples where this still happens.

You know that old saying about those who don't learn from history being doomed to repeat it? For all the benefits of the church, we sometimes have selective amnesia when it comes to remembering where we came from.

Some religious leaders will say you can't be a Christian without claiming the perfect, inerrant authority of scripture. The good news is that you get to decide for yourself whether you agree with them or not.

. . . .

Joshua Toulouse

A. The Bible says that all scripture is inspired by God, or it can be translated as "breathed" or "spirited" by God. But nowhere do the scriptures claim to be handed down directly from God without possibility

5

for error. While some traditions have understood scripture this way, it is certainly not a requirement for Christianity.

I choose to see the idea that scripture is inspired by God to mean that God inspired the writing of the scripture but also respected the humanity of those who were doing the writing. God recognizes that we are not perfect, and therefore nothing we create will be perfect either.

It is helpful to consider too that the inspiration of God regarding scripture doesn't end when the writing is complete. God is also inspiring those of us who hear or read scripture today. With this understanding, God is kept active in scripture, in that scripture can speak to us in new ways and on different levels now as opposed to when it was written.

The breathing or spiriting of God in scripture occurs today, just as much in our receiving of scripture as it was in the writing.

....

Becky Garrison

A. This concept of reading the Bible line by line is a relatively new way of interpreting scripture that would have been totally foreign to pre-Enlightenment Christians. Even the most die-hard literalist acknowledges that when Jesus was speaking in parables, his audience knew that he was using metaphors and symbols.

To reduce the poetry, metaphor, symbolism, and other literary devices present in this holy book to a point where the Bible becomes a technical how-to manual misses the mystery behind the myriad ways that God has spoken to humanity throughout history.

....

Jim L. Robinson

A. Of course! Christianity is not based on one's affirmation of scripture or the correctness of one's doctrine; rather, it's based on God's grace and our trust in that grace.

I don't buy the exact description of "inerrancy" that's such a crucial belief for some Christians. On the other hand, I believe that any perceived "errors" are not really in scripture but in human presuppositions about the texts.

The Bible is a human witness to the presence and grace of God. God interacts with humans and sometimes (by way of divine inspiration) some humans get it. They perceive and understand that presence and write down their experience. Down through history some of those writings have been collected to provide a standard by which succeeding generations can evaluate their own experiences.

As to "handed down directly from God," that's again a matter of definition. Yes, I believe that God is the source of the truth in scripture, but I don't believe that God dictated it word for word. The truth and the validity of the Christian witness are proven in the arena of history where God interacts with humans. We are known by the fruits we bear.

· · · · · ·

Scriptural References

Matthew 7:24–29; 28:19; Mark 1:21–28; Luke 24:13–32; 2 Timothy 3:15–16; 2 Peter 1:20–21

Suggested Additional Sources for Reading

- Paul J. Achtemeier, *Inspiration and Authority: Nature and Function of Christian Scripture* (Hendrickson, 1999).
- Karen Armstrong, *The Case for God* (Alfred A. Knopf, 2009).
- Marcus J. Borg, *The God We Never Knew: Beyond Dogmatic Religion to a More Authentic Contemporary Faith* (HarperOne, 1997), especially chap. 7, "Salvation: What on Earth Do We Mean?"
- Marcus J. Borg, *The Heart of Christianity: Rediscovering a Life of Faith* (HarperOne, 2003), especially chap. 3, "The Bible: The Heart of the Tradition."
- Ed Cyzewski, *Coffeehouse Theology* (NavPress, 2008).
- Bart D. Ehrman, *Jesus, Interrupted: Revealing the Hidden Contradictions in the Bible (and Why We Don't Know about Them)* (HarperOne, 2010).
- Bart D. Ehrman, *Misquoting Jesus: The Story behind Who Changed the Bible and Why* (HarperOne, 2007).
- Daniel Erlander, *Baptized, We Live: Lutheranism as a Way of Life* (Augsburg Fortress Press, 1995).
- Peter J. Gomes, *The Scandalous Gospel of Jesus: What's So Good about the Good News?* (HarperOne, 2007), especially "Introduction" and chap. 1, "We Start with the Bible."
- Joel B. Green, *Salvation* (Chalice Press 2003).
- N. T. Wright, *The Last Word: Scripture and the Authority of God—Getting beyond the Bible Wars* (HarperOne, 2006).

Suggested Questions for Further Discussion/Thought

1. If you are saved by the Bible's lack of errors, what happens if you find a mistake in it?

2. How deep are you willing to go in Bible study? Are you willing to consider sources other than those that support what you already think you believe?

3. What kind of relationship should Christians have with the Bible?

4. Joel Green defines salvation as "God drawing near." How do you define salvation?

5. What makes someone Christian?

Aren't women treated poorly throughout the Bible? Why would any intelligent modern woman today even want to read the Bible?

Rebecca Bowman Woods

Growing up in the church, I learned the better-known stories of biblical women. By age ten or eleven, I had a few questions, such as: Why was Jacob allowed to marry both Rachel and Leah? Why was it such a big deal to be "barren"? Why didn't Jesus have any female disciples (or did he)? And was Eve really to blame for . . . everything?

By the time I discovered the really awful Old Testament stories and the New Testament texts commanding women to be silent in church, cover their heads, and obey their husbands, I wanted nothing to do with the Bible, or frankly, with Christianity.

What convinced me was reading about Jesus. Even though the gospel writers were male, it's clear that Jesus had an ethic of equality when it came to women. They supported his ministry and were among his closest friends. He rescued a woman caught in adultery from death by public stoning and then convinced her that her soul was worth saving, too. Some of his longest conversations in scripture were with women. When most of the disciples went into hiding on Good Friday, the women stayed by the cross, and women were the first to see the risen Jesus.

A closer look at the rest of the Bible shows a steady (if not sparse) line of women who played a role in God's unfolding story. Alongside the "good girls" whose names I learned in Sunday School are those who challenged the status quo, made the best of bad situations, and followed God's call to service, leadership, and ministry: Tamar, Deborah, Bathsheba, Esther, Mary Magdalene, Mary and Martha, Joanna, Lydia, and Priscilla. These and nameless others demonstrate resourcefulness, strength, and courage—all the more remarkable considering their place in ancient culture.

Becky Garrison

While tradition tends to accord Mary with having found favored status with God (Lk. 1:26–38), let us not forget the women around Jesus who kicked some holy hiney. For example, Anna, the only woman designated a prophet in the New Testament, possessed the wisdom and foresight to see that this infant before her represented the Messiah (Lk. 2:36–38).

If Jesus truly wanted women stuck in the kitchen, he wouldn't have encouraged Mary to join the other disciples in their discussions. Instead, he would have encouraged her to hang back washing dishes (Lk. 10:38–42). Furthermore, when Jesus was told his family was looking for him, he replied, "Here are my mother and my brothers!" (Mk. 3:31–35). He would not have said "mother" had there not been females as part of his entourage.

All throughout his ministry, Jesus debunked the first-century Jewish tradition that treated women like property. His actions with the Samaritan woman at the well (Jn. 4:4–26), the woman about to be stoned for adultery (Jn. 8:1–12), and the female sinner who wanted to anoint his feet with oil (Lk. 7:36–50) marked him as a man who would break every holy law on the books so that women could be viewed as equals in the kingdom of God.

Let us also not forget that Jesus made his very first appearance as the risen Lord before a "lowly" woman (Mk. 16:9 and Jn. 20:11–18).

. . . .

Craig Detweiler

A The ancient world was quite patriarchal. Women were rarely afforded the rights and equality we've all come to accept as natural and God-given. Plenty of examples of abuse are found in the Jewish scriptures. Eve is blamed for original sin. Women are rarely counted in ancient censuses. They are not given power, property, or even a voice. In a particularly haunting New Testament passage, the apostle Paul insists, "As in all the churches of the saints, women should be silent in the churches. For they are not permitted to speak, but should be subordinate, as the law also says. If there is anything they desire to know, let them ask their husbands at home. For it is shameful for a woman to speak in church" (1 Cor. 14:34–35).

So why read the Bible? Women may find themselves strangely moved by Jesus' relationship with the opposite sex. He goes out of his way to affirm the value of women who have seemingly been discarded by their culture. Jesus defends the woman caught in adultery. He pauses to refresh the woman at the well. He stops for a women suffering from an issue of blood. He heals Jairus' daughter. He responds to the cries of Mary and Martha by resurrecting their beloved Lazarus.

If women find themselves discouraged by the ghosts of a patriarchal past, they may find Jesus a surprisingly liberating figure. He upsets the status quo by addressing women, affirming women, and befriending women, regardless of their social status.

....
Marcia Ford

Many—but not all—ancient cultures were patriarchal societies in which men had all the power and women were treated as possessions. While there were exceptions throughout its history, most notably the elevation of Deborah to the position of judge, Israelite society perpetuated that structure. While some see the Bible as condoning masculine control, others interpret the biblical perpetuation of patriarchy as a way of working within existing cultural norms.

This background is what makes Jesus' attitude toward women so astonishing. Jesus healed, delivered, and saved women as well as men and never discouraged women from following him. There's evidence that the women who traveled with Jesus were largely responsible for underwriting his ministry. Women were treated as valuable human beings, every bit as worthwhile
as men.

Those who see the Bible as misogynistic often interpret Paul's teachings limiting the role of women as representative of all of scripture. But they fail to realize how much responsibility women had in the early church and how much the male followers of Jesus—including Paul—relied on women to provide for their ministries and even correct those who misunderstood the gospel, as Priscilla did.

Intelligent women today have much to learn from the Bible once they grasp the stunning message Jesus brought to the women of his day. Never before had anyone, especially a religious leader, offered them the hope and promise of a new way of living that Jesus did.

• • • • • •

Scriptural References

Luke 1:26–38; 2:36–38; 7:36–50; 10:38–42; Mark 3:31–35; 16:9; John 4:4–26; 8:1–12; 20:11–18; Acts 2:17; 18:24–28; Joel 2:28–29; Galatians 3:28; Matthew 26:13; Judges 4:4; 5:7, 31

Suggested Additional Sources for Reading

- Kenneth E. Bailey, *Jesus through Middle Eastern Eyes* (IVP Academic, 2008).

- John T. Bristow, *What Paul Really Said about Women: The Apostle's Liberating Views on Equality in Marriage, Leadership, and Love* (HarperOne, 1991).

- Christians for Biblical Equality: http://www.cbeinternational.org.

- Loren Cunningham, David Joel Hamilton, and Janice Rogers, *Why Not Women: A Biblical Study of Women in Missions, Ministry, and Leadership* (YWAM Publishers, 2000).

- J. Lee Grady, *10 Lies the Church Tells Women and 25 Tough Questions About Women and the Church* (Charisma House, 2006).
- Stanley J. Grenz and Denise Muir Kjesbo, *Women in the Church: A Biblical Theology of Women in Ministry* (IVP Academic, 1995).
- Liz Curtis Higgs, *Bad Girls of the Bible and What We Can Learn from Them* (WaterBrook, 1999).
- Craig S. Keener, *Paul, Women, and Wives: Marriage and Women's Ministry in the Letters of Paul* (Hendrickson, 1992).
- Virginia Stem Owen, *Daughters of Eve: Seeing Ourselves in Women of the Bible* (NavPress, 1995).
- Lisa Wolfe, *Uppity Women of the Bible* (Four DVD set, available at http://www.livingthequestions.com).

Suggested Questions for Further Discussion/Thought

1. How do contemporary Christian women reclaim the legacies of Anna and Mary Magdalene?
2. How has your church used the Bible to either promote women in ministry or deny them participation in meaningful ministry?
3. Imagine being a first-century woman in Palestine who has only known a life dominated by men. What kind of impact do you think Jesus' teachings would have had on you?
4. Matthew 1:1–17, the genealogy of Jesus, includes four women: Tamar, Rahab, Ruth, and Bathsheba (called the wife of Uriah). Locate, read, and discuss these women's stories in the Old Testament. What do they have in common? Why do you think the gospel writer included them in the genealogy of Jesus?
5. Are women better off today than in ancient times?

How can a God be all-loving yet allow people to be thrown into hell?

Jarrod McKenna

The Bible doesn't say God is all-loving. In my work heading up an interfaith youth organization in Western Australia, I have often heard my Muslim friends speak of the ninety-nine beautiful names of Allah, including *Al Wadud*, "The Loving One." The Bible, however, makes a claim not just about an attribute of God but about the mysterious unknowable essence of the Holy Triune God—that God is not just loving, but that "God IS love" (1 Jn. 4:8).

The context of this verse is very important in responding to the question of hell. "Whoever does not love does not know God, for God is love." Jesus not only reveals God fully but also reveals what it is to be fully human. You don't need to be a historian to know that it's hell when we reject God by living like we were made in the image of something other than the Love revealed in Jesus (1 Jn. 4:9–12). Tolstoy wrote, "Where love is, God is also." It's equally true to say "Where Love is not—that's hell."

Any talk of hell must come in the narrative of the Creator who has acted decisively to redeem all of creation, uniting heaven and earth in the nonviolent Messiah Jesus. We were made by Love, in the image of Love, to participate in the dance that flows between the Holy Trinity that is Love and that we see fully revealed in Jesus to be Love, and this Love will one day cover the earth "as the waters cover the sea" (Isa. 11:9).

To not eternally be fully human by participating in the dance of Love that is God is . . . hell. Hell is what happens when we willingly decide to collaborate with the dehumanizing forces of violence, injustice, and misery that will be no more when love is "all in all" (1 Cor. 15:28). That is why C. S. Lewis could write, "Hell's gates are locked from the inside."

Jim L. Robinson

One explanation is that people make their own choices and reap the consequences. The rules are clear and there are no excuses. Another response would suggest that "hell" is the extension of a primitive reward-and-punishment worldview that is not really consistent with later writings in the New Testament.

The bottom line is that none of us knows the mind of God. We walk by faith, not by sight. No matter what we conclude, there is no guarantee that we're "right." Unfortunately, there are those who spout teachings about grace but who still believe you have to "get it right" if you want to go to heaven. It's not grace if we have to do anything to get it.

Whatever I say is a statement of faith, not of knowledge. If we knew, there'd be no need for faith. Indeed, from one perspective, the opposite of faith is not doubt but knowledge; and if the New Testament is clear on anything, it is that we are justified by and through faith.

Personally, I prefer to err on the side of grace rather than rules, laws, and prerequisites. I find in scripture a movement away from law and toward grace.

I believe, projecting on the basis of that movement, that God does not "allow people to be thrown into hell." I'm relatively confident that present-day teachings about hell will one day be revealed as a human misinterpretation of scripture—either in the writing, in the reading, or in both. However, that is a statement of faith, not of knowledge.

• • • • • •

Scriptural References

Isaiah 11:9; 1 Corinthians 15:28; 1 John 4:8–12

Suggested Additional Source for Reading

- N. T. Wright, *For All the Saints?* (Morehouse, 2004).

Suggested Questions for Further Discussion/Thought

1. What is grace? Are there prerequisites to receiving grace? If there are prerequisites, is it really grace?

2. Can one "fall" from grace? How?

3. Do you believe in hell? What informs your understanding of it?

What does the Bible really say about homosexuality?

Christian Piatt

A. Perhaps nothing sparks more heated debate over scripture than the biblical position on homosexuality. First off, it should be pointed out that there is no reference whatsoever in any biblical scripture to homosexuality; rather, scripture refers in some instances to homosexual acts. Depending on your understanding of sexual orientation, there can be a big difference between the two.

The story of Sodom and Gomorrah is perhaps the most famous—or infamous—but it's important to understand how homosexual behavior was used in the town from which the term "sodomy" was coined. When a town was conquered, one way that the victorious army would demonstrate their dominance was to rape the women of the village. Sometimes, to add further insult to the defeat, they would even rape the men.

Rather than an intimate act, this behavior actually was a military strategy, though brutal and repulsive, to break the spirits of the defeated culture.

Other references, including those by the apostle Paul, condemn men for lying with men as if they are women. Again, some context helps us understand that certain non-Christian religions of the time conducted ritual orgies as a tribute to their god or gods, and though it can be argued either way, it's possible that Paul was referring to what he considered a heathenish religious practice rather than consensual gay sex.

Jesus never spoke about homosexuality or homosexual acts, so for those who look principally to him for guidance, we're left with our own consciences to guide us.

Kathy Escobar

A. The passages that are commonly used as an argument against homosexuality are Romans 1:26–27, 1 Corinthians 6:9–10, and Leviticus 18:22 and 20:13.

However, like all the translations of the Bible, there are many kinds of different meanings that can be drawn from the original words that people use to prove their divergent points. In the 1 Corinthians 6 passage, for example, which is often used, the word for "homosexual offenders"— *arsenokoitai*—has a wide range of interpretations.

That is one of the crazy parts about being more honest about Bible interpretation; it is subjective and always open for scrutiny if we respect our human limitations and inability to be 100 percent certain what God means. Regarding this issue, it is interesting that Jesus was never recorded in the gospels as mentioning homosexuality, yet clearly this has become one of the most significantly "Christian" issues of our time.

I come from a conservative evangelical tradition and have made great shifts in what I believe over the years as I began to realize that I primarily believed certain things because that was what people in power told me. As I started to do my own biblical research (and cultivate close relationships with gay and lesbian friends), my heart began to feel far less certain about what I had been taught. Because my church, The Refuge, is an inclusive community, sometimes people of a more conservative persuasion will ask me, "What we do about the gay people who are part of our community? Don't we tell them the truth about what the Bible says?"

My answer has become so clear and freeing. I tell them, "I know that you see the scriptures that way, and I understand there are some passages in the Bible that point to homosexual behavior as a sin, but it would be a good idea for you to know some other people who see those passages differently, who read the same exact words as you and have solid convictions—as solid as yours—that are completely different from your viewpoint. Maybe you can learn from each other in true community instead of arguing over the teaching of biblical truth."

Over time, I have come to the conclusion that I don't really know, but I don't really need to know. I don't have a simple way to reconcile these passages or dismiss created design and the differences between male and female anatomy. Regardless, I can say that all of the unknowns, various interpretations, and perspectives do force me to keep turning to and relying on the bigger story, and the bigger story is about Jesus alive and at work, restoring, rebuilding, healing, challenging, moving people of all shapes, sizes, colors, and sexual orientations.

....

Joshua Einsohn

The Bible says a lot of pretty mean things about homosexuality: "You shall not lie with a male as with a woman; it is an abomination" (Lev. 18:22). (I know that the Lord was speaking with Moses here, but the subtle sexism should be noted . . . it overlooks woman-on-woman action.)

Leviticus goes back for more: "If a man lies with a male as with a woman, both of them have committed an abomination; they shall be put to death; their blood is upon them" (Lev. 20:13).

And lest we forget the New Testament, Romans 1:26–27 says that men and women who have homosexual relations are considered "unnatural" and pretty much have it comin' for their "perversion." Nice to see that women were acknowledged here, though. Progress of a sort, I suppose.

However, there are many laws that aren't followed today because they are considered antiquated or irrelevant. In Leviticus 19:20, it says that it's OK to doink a slave girl as long as she hasn't been freed and you feel pretty crappy about it afterwards. And there's also: "All who curse father or mother shall be put to death" (Lev. 20:9). I'm sure that the parents of many teenagers are game for that one, but modern law prohibits it and that's probably a good idea. We see very few stonings these days that aren't frowned upon, but it was quite the fad back then.

Many ancient laws, from keeping kosher to circumcision, are considered up for interpretation. Pro-gay-rights advocates claim that there have been mistranslations and inconsistent enforcement of laws. Many conservatives argue that these passages should be adhered to strictly.

All I know is that when I hear these words hurled at me and people that I care about, they hurt. A lot.

....

Jason Boyett

The Bible explicitly condemns homosexuality, but these few passages leave room for interpretation. For example, Genesis 19—the destruction of Sodom and Gomorrah—is traditionally thought to have been a punishment on the cities' rampant homosexuality. After all, that's where we got the term "sodomites." But Ezekiel 16:49 says the sin of Sodom was arrogance, apathy, and neglect of the poor. So was God punishing Sodom for homosexuality in general? For something specific like rape or inhospitality? Or for something else?

Likewise, Leviticus 18:22 and 20:13 describe "[lying] with a male as one lies with a woman" as "an abomination." Seems pretty clear, right? But it also describes sex with a woman during her period as being an abomination. These verses are part of a holiness code to separate the Israelites from neighboring cultures. Some scholars suggest it doesn't condemn a homosexual lifestyle as much as it prohibits a specific pagan temple practice.

What about the New Testament? Romans 1:26–27 identifies homosexual activity as "degrading," but the passage seems to address ritual behavior or pagan orgies. First Corinthians 6:9–10 denies God's kingdom to "homosexual offenders," based on a confusing Greek word that probably refers to older customers of young male prostitutes (pederasty).

What's the point? The Bible condemns specific homosexual acts, but doesn't address what we typically think of as homosexuality today—homosexual orientation or loving, committed homosexual relationships. This doesn't mean the Bible approves of it but only that it is silent on the subject.

Joshua Toulouse

A. There are two mentions in the book of Leviticus that say it is wrong for males to lie with males as if they were female, and these mentions sit alongside rules that say you cannot wear clothing made of two different materials. There are many laws in Leviticus that we don't feel apply to us now, and yet this one is still given credence by those that would condemn homosexuality.

In Corinthians and Timothy, two of the most cited examples of the Bible being against homosexuality, the real problem is one of translation. The word used is *arsenokoites*, which is only used in these two books. It has been translated in many places as either "homosexual" or "sodomite," and yet these are not clear translations for the word. Looking at the context, it is far more likely that these words have to do with sexual exploitation of some kind—either prostitution or rape—and not consensual sex.

In Romans, the issue is not homosexuality, but rather idolatry. Paul is pointing out to his readers the dangers of committing idolatry, and part of that is giving into lustful behavior. Paul looks at males lying with males and females lying with females as being outside of natural behavior, and therefore being solely driven by lust, because at the time there was no understanding of sexual orientation.

José F. Morales Jr.

A. What does the Bible say about homosexuality as we understand it today—as an orientation, not simply as a choice? Nothing. Well, maybe something.

In the Levitical Code (Lev. 17–26), homosexuality is called an abomination, but so is eating shrimp and wearing mixed fabric. But we somehow don't get our cotton-blend panties in a bunch whenever we go to Red Lobster. We highlight one verse about "homosexuality" and ignore the rest, and have wrongfully used it to discriminate against homosexuals. Interestingly, most scholars admit that these verses are some of the hardest to translate and understand.

Then comes Paul. Paul reduces homosexuality to pederasty (men using boys) and cultic male prostitution. He had no concept of faithful, monogamous, same-sex relationships or of sexual orientation. Therefore, the Bible says nothing about homosexuality as we under . . .

But wait! Christian biologist Joan Roughgarden argues that we're looking in the wrong place. She says we need to see how the Bible treats eunuchs, for the term "eunuch" also referred to "effeminate" men, men with both sets of genitals, and men with same-sex attraction. This last one comes closest to contemporary understanding: "For some are eunuchs because they were born that way" (Mt. 19:12).

In the Law, eunuchs are condemned. But in Acts 8, a eunuch is baptized by Philip and portrayed in the text, and in later Ethiopian church tradition, as a righteous leader in the church.

And most powerfully, in Isaiah 56:4–5, 8,

"To the eunuchs who keep my sabbaths,
who choose the things that please me . . .
I will give, within my house and within my walls.
a monument and a name . . .
I will give them an everlasting name . . .
I will gather others to them besides those already gathered."

God is gathering the gays . . . awesome!

· · · · · ·

Scriptural References

Genesis 19; Leviticus 18:22; 20:13; 19:20; 20:9; Ezekiel 16:49; Romans 1:26–27; 1 Corinthians 6:9–10; Isaiah 56:1–8; Acts 8:26–40; 1 Timothy 1:10

Suggested Additional Sources for Reading

- AllorNotAtAll: http://www.ALLorNotAtAll.org/resources.

- John Boswell, *Christianity, Social Tolerance, and Homosexuality: Gay People in Western Europe from the Beginning of the Christian Era to the Fourteenth Century* (Univ. of Chicago Press, 2008).

- Martin Copenhaver and Anthony Robinson, *Words for the Journey: Letters to Our Teenagers about Life and Faith* (Pilgrim Press, 2003), especially chap. 34, "Homosexuality."

- Evangelicals Concerned: http://www.ecwr.org.

- *For the Bible Tells Me So*, film, 99 minutes, VisionQuest/Atticus Group, 2007.

- Sally B. Geis and Donald E. Messer, *Caught in the Crossfire: Helping Christians Debate Homosexuality* (Abingdon Press, 1994).

- Peter J. Gomes, *The Good Book: Reading the Bible with Mind and Heart* (HarperOne, 2002), especially chap. 8, "The Bible and Homosexuality: The Last Prejudice."

- Daniel A. Helminiak, *What the Bible Really Says about Homosexuality: Explode the Myths, Heal the Church* (Westminster John Knox Press, 2009).

- Andrew P. Marin, *Love Is an Orientation: Elevating the Conversation with the Gay Community* (InterVarsity Press, 2009).
- Religious Tolerance: http://www.religioustolerance.org.
- Jack Barlett Rogers, *Jesus, the Bible, and Homosexuality* (Westminster John Knox Press, 2009).
- Joan Roughgarden, *Evolution and Christian Faith: Reflections of an Evolutionary Biologist* (Island Press, 2006), especially chap. 11, "Gender and Sexuality."
- Soulforce: http://www.soulforce.org.
- David K. Switzer, *Pastoral Care of Gays, Lesbians, and Their Families* (Augsburg Fortress, 1999).
- Mary Ann Tolbert, "A New Teaching with Authority: A Re-evaluation of the Authority of the Bible," The Progressive Christian Witness: http://www.progressivechristianwitness.org/pcw/pdf/Tolbert_NewTeaching.pdf.
- Mel White, *What the Bible Says—and Doesn't Say—about Homosexuality* (Soulforce, 2007).
- Garry Wills, *What Jesus Meant* (Penguin, 2006), especially chap. 2, "The Work Begins."

Suggested Questions for Further Discussion/Thought

1. The Bible is much more forthright in its prohibitions against divorce; Jesus calls it "adultery" when divorced people remarry. Why, then, does homosexuality carry such a stigma in the church if divorce does not?
2. Read Romans 1:24–27. Paul was unaware of the notion of sexual orientation; therefore he speaks of "unnatural" homosexual relations. If we accept homosexuality, like heterosexuality, as orientation (i.e., as "natural"), does this change the way we interpret these verses? If so, how should we interpret this passage today?
3. In attempting to discuss the biblical view concerning homosexuality, what are the strengths and weaknesses of using the "eunuch" approach discussed earlier?
4. Do you know someone who is gay and a devoted Christian? What are you learning from them?
6. Do you believe homosexuality is a sin? Why or why not? What would it mean to let go of the need to be clear on this issue?
7. Do you believe homosexuality is genetic, environmental, or some combination of both? Explain.

Why haven't any new books been added to the Bible in almost two thousand years? Is there a chance any new books will ever be added? Why or why not?

Joshua Einsohn

Considering the level of healthy skepticism and the wealth of knowledge that exists now that didn't exist two thousand years ago, it's highly unlikely that we'll be seeing any additions to the Bible.

We have science now and we can explain way too much for much of anything to seem like a miracle anymore. There's also way too much information out there; we can find out anything about anyone and at some point, we'd find out that a new potential prophet has a "nanny problem" or that they slept with a church member of the same sex or one of the myriad of reasons that previously reputable people are thrown under the proverbial bus.

Also, let's imagine for one minute that a well-respected member of society were to go up a mountain and come back down with new, crazy-sounding laws that they got from a shrub that was on fire.

Uh-huh.

Most of us would back away slowly and call the men with the pretty white jackets that have all those straps and buckles. Of the people who remained, a few would be potential believers. The rest would just want to know where they got the amazing weed.

The mystery and mythology of history has given the Bible it's "cred" and it would take a global communication crisis of apocalyptic proportions before that would change.

Gary Peluso-Verdend

The early years of any religious movement are fluid. Over time, movements gel into institutions—or the movements and their purposes cease. The early gelling of Christianity included separating from Judaism (Christianity began as a Jewish reform movement) and distinguishing "orthodox" Christianity (right belief and practice) from heterodoxy or heresy. What became orthodox Christianity might also be understood as the victor in the battle against Montanists and Gnostics, to name two of the most prominent heterodox groups.

In the gelling process, the church developed creeds and a canon of scripture. Creeds, such as the Nicene, became a powerful measure of who was a heretic. The word "canon" means "measure" or "rule." Settling on a canon of scripture was one way the churches' teaching authorities tried to define authentic Christian belief and practice.

In modern times, scholars have subjected all truth claims to historical tests, including the claims of those who believed God led them to accept books as canonical. Even before the modern period, however, notable theologians disputed which books should be included in the canon. Martin Luther famously wrote that James is an epistle "stuffed with straw," and he did not believe that Revelation preached Christ.

I do not think the canon will ever be reopened. Once closed, a canon accumulates a history of usage that makes it more difficult than at the outset of the canon to add or delete a text. Also, in our present age, it is impossible to imagine an agreed-upon process, with agreed-upon representatives authorized to choose another writing that would be affirmed by all as word of God, report of the word of God, or reflection of the Word of God.

I cannot imagine such an effort producing anything other than headlines and grief.

· ·

José F. Morales Jr.

A Some believe that the Bible is closed, that no more books may be added. They base this argument on the warning in Revelation: "I warn everyone who hears the words of the prophecy of this book: If anyone adds to them, God will add to that person the plagues described in this book" (Rev. 22:18). Yet "this book" clearly refers to Revelation and not to the whole canon.

"Canon" refers to the standard collection of books accepted by "the church." Interestingly, to this day, the "canon" is contested within the church universal: Protestants, Catholics, Syriac Orthodox, and Chaldeans all have assembled ("canonized") slightly different collections. For example, the Church of the East (Chaldean) only accepts twenty-two books in the New Testament, whereas Protestants accept twenty-seven.

Nowhere within the Bible are there any specifications on what to include and how. And nowhere does the Bible "close" itself from addition. So we can feasibly say that books theoretically may be added. Shortly after the 1960s, some Christians in America and elsewhere considered canonizing "The Letter from Birmingham Jail" by Martin Luther King Jr. After all, it did have epistle-like qualities. Yet I think the consensus within the church is to leave it as is. (We're still trying to make sense of the books we have. Why add to the drama?)

This we can be sure of: We received these sacred texts, however assembled, as a gift from the ancients of our respective traditions—an imperfect yet wonderful gift to guide us in our journey. Our forebears collected these books because their hearts were stirred by the words in their pages and because they wished the same stirring upon the hearts of their children.

....

Marcia Ford

There are several reasons why new books have not been added to the Bible, the first and foremost of which is the prevailing belief that in the sixty-six books of the Bible, God has provided all that we need to know to believe in God and to guide our lives. A second reason is "the apostolic principle," that is, that the books of the New Testament must be related to the life or ministry of an apostle. This simply has not been possible since the second century. Based on the second reason alone, there would be no chance that new books would be added to the canon of scripture.

There's also the warning in Revelation 22:18–19, which applies to the book of Revelation but which many have expanded to apply to the entire Bible. It warns people not to add to or subtract from "the words of this book." But even many of those who apply those verses to just the book of Revelation would never presume to alter the Bible as a whole.

Remember, too, that there's no longer any central church authority that could make such a decision. As scattered as the early church was, Jesus' followers were nonetheless in communication with each other and with the bishops who essentially placed their stamp of approval on the books the churches were already using—books that now compose the New Testament. There is no such authority in place today.

....

Joshua Toulouse

The process of finalizing the books in the Bible took hundreds of years and was by no means an overnight decision. But since the canon was ratified in the year 397 in Carthage, the matter has been closed. There are still differences among religious groups on exactly what is and is not canon, but there is no possibility of any new books being added. The books that are in the Bible were chosen because they were used consistently by many church communities and were largely universally considered as relevant and authoritative.

Although the canon was not ratified until the late fourth century, there were many proposals of a canon prior to that point. In most of them, the books mentioned as deserving of consideration as scripture are often very close, if not identical, to the books that we now view as the Bible. So even though there were some books that some groups felt should be included yet were not, and some books that groups felt shouldn't be included that were, for the most part the Bible we have now has been used for most of the last two thousand years.

Because of this shared history of communities viewing these books as scripture, nothing added now would have the same historical importance to the church as the books in the Bible. While other Christian writings can and do gain importance for various communities, recognition as actual scripture requires a tradition of acceptance throughout the history of the church as a component and that is something that no new book can have.

• • • • • •

Scriptural References

Jeremiah 31:32–34; Romans 15:4; 2 Timothy 3:14–17; Revelation 22:18–19

Suggested Additional Sources for Reading

- Craig D. Allert, *A High View of Scripture? The Authority of the Bible and the Formation of the New Testament Canon* (Baker Academic, 2007).
- Karen Armstrong, *The Bible: A Biography* (Grove, 2008).
- Luke Timothy Johnson, *The Writings of the New Testament: An Interpretation* (Fortress Press, 2002), especially the epilogue.
- Lee Martin McDonald, *The Biblical Canon: Its Origin, Transmission, and Authority* (Hendrickson, 2007).
- Bruce M. Metzger and Michael D. Coogan, eds., *Oxford Guide to the Bible* (Oxford Univ. Press, 2004), especially "Canon" by Andrie B. du Toit.
- Jaroslav Pelikan, *Whose Bible Is It? A Short History of the Scriptures* (Penguin, 2005).

Suggested Questions for Further Discussion/Thought

1. Do you think the Bible is open or closed for additions? Why?
2. If you believe the Bible is open, what criteria should be used to determine whether a book is "scripture worthy"?
3. Would a global holocaust allow room for new books in the Bible to be written? Would society be coherent enough to spread the new Word? Or would the total unraveling of communication that allowed for the emotional possibility of more books being written prevent those same documents from being disseminated?
4. Some readers of the gnostic gospels believe that such books as the gospel of Thomas, the gospel of Mary, and the Secret Book of James should be added to the New Testament. What do you think of this idea? Who would be responsible for making such a decision?
5. What books, if any, do you consider to be on a par with scripture?

Did God write the Bible? If so, why didn't God simply create it miraculously, rather than using so many people over thousands of years to write it down?

....

Gary Peluso-Verdend

I once saw a cartoon that pictured God (depicted as a male) in the heavens with a megaphone. Tubes extended from the megaphone to the earth, where four men sat at typewriters reproducing at the keys the words they were hearing. The cartoonist was trying, positively, to express the claim that the four gospel writers were transmitting what they heard from God, word for word.

I think the Bible is an inspired text but not in the way portrayed in the cartoon.

From one of the opening stories in the Bible—Adam and Eve—we learn that God chooses to work through and with human agents. One could argue that God could care directly for widows and orphans, feed the hungry, and house the sojourner. Instead, God chooses to work through us.

So it is with the scriptures. I believe God inspired persons and communities over the nearly two thousand years of history contained in the Bible. They were inspired with ideas and stories, with laws and morals and values, and with an understanding of a God whose character is love and who has created humankind to reflect the divine character.

When writers recorded the pieces that other writers and scribes stitched together over time into what today is our Bible, they included the words of God, the hopes and dreams and anger of their own communities, their insights, and both their cultural biases and their wounds.

What we have in the Bible is a community of interpreters of the word of God. It is exciting and challenging, in our day as in any day, to join that community and to dare our interpretations.

....

José F. Morales Jr.

Short answer: No. God did inspire it, but did not write it (2 Tim. 3:16).

God used peoples and communities over time to give birth and breath to what we now call "the Bible." Before the written word was the spoken word, that is, oral stories and traditions that were transmitted within Israel and the early church. Israel understood its holy identity through these oral traditions: stories of creation and election (Genesis), of liberation (Exodus) and instruction (the Law), and of adoration (Psalms) and proclamation (the prophets).

These stories and some new ones shaped the early church: incarnation (the gospels) and mission (Acts and the epistles). So the Bible is a collection of the people's encounter with a God who creates, redeems, judges, and restores.

The oral stories were not committed to writing until something terrible happened. The Jews were deported to Babylon, and the Temple destroyed. These displaced and distraught exiles needed somewhere new around which to gather, being that they no longer had the Temple.

Over time, observance of "the Law and the Prophets" became a way to recreate a "temple" of sorts. And by writing it down, this "temple" of oral tradition was given concrete permanence. The gospels came about in a similar way, but within a shorter time span.

Christians adopted this notion of the "temple" being whenever and wherever the faithful gathered around the word. And they did this because whenever they engaged the written word, they sensed that they were encountering the Living Word, Jesus. "For where two or three are gathered in my name, I am there among them" (Mt. 18:20).

The Bible shapes us because its stories are our stories and because we encounter Jesus along the way.

....
Kathy Escobar

I believe God used people to write the Bible. Through divine inspiration, the words were recorded. At the same time, I do not believe they appear in the many translations of the Bible that I have on my bookshelf in the exact way they were originally. I think pastors and leaders must become more honest about that.

Translation always leaves room for human error, and despite that possibility, it doesn't affect my extremely high view of the transforming power of the Bible. I love how God can use the flawed to reveal the perfect. I have absolutely no idea why God didn't just magically make the words appear in a neat and tidy package, but my guess is that even if God had done it that way, the same things would be up for grabs when it comes to interpretation and haggling over what it means and says.

Using a diverse mix of people from a wide variety of backgrounds over a long period of time seems to be more God's style.

The quick, simple, homogenous way we long for is extremely inconsistent with most honest issues of faith. God's obsession with using "people" is fairly apparent, so it makes sense to me that the story would be told through them. And it would leave us with holes that only faith, as described in Hebrews 11, could fill.

....
Joshua Toulouse

We are told in the Bible that all scripture is from God. It is usually translated as "inspired" by God, but the literal translation is "breathed" or "spirited" by God. However you translate the word, it doesn't say that God wrote the Bible.

Still, it is clear that we are to believe that God had an active role in the creation of the Bible. So even if God didn't literally write the Bible, the question is still valid: Why was it written by so many people over thousands of years?

While the Bible is bound for us in the modern era as one book, each of the writings in their original context was written for specific reasons and to meet specific needs. They were chosen as canonical scripture because they were seen to serve more than their original function. The writings spoke to believers in other contexts and in other times and continued to be used liturgically in worship or for teaching. But first and foremost, they served a particular need that would not have been met if the Bible had been handed down complete from heaven, written by God.

While these writings were meant for a specific time in a particular situation, the active participation of God, through breath/spirit/inspiration, has made them applicable to the religious community beyond that specific time or those particular situations.

....
Jim L. Robinson

I know of no credible person or source that would say God "wrote" the Bible. A much more common description of the origin of scripture focuses on the word "inspired." A common understanding of inspiration might be characterized as an angel perching on Paul's shoulder dictating directly into Paul's ear the words of his epistle to the Philippians. Some understandings basically remove all traces of human influence or participation in the writing of scripture.

I believe the Bible is divinely inspired. I do not define inspired as "verbally, one-word-at-a-time dictated." In my understanding, God inspires (breathes into) a person or a community an acute and accurate understanding of the meaning of God's intention in any event or occasion. My reading of scripture is more concerned with overall meaning than with verbal accuracy.

Divine inspiration does not bypass human vocabulary and thought patterns. Truth is truth, no matter what the medium may be. Its communication is concerned as much about what is heard as what is said. In other words, if I say something that you don't understand, then there is no value in my saying it.

In order to be effective in communication, God conveys meaning to people and communities in their language and cultural contexts. They, in turn, communicate that meaning in their own language and contexts.

It is impossible to communicate the fullness of God in human language. God surpasses all attempts at human description. It often becomes necessary to use metaphor and hyperbole in communicating the understandings that God inspires. The Bible is full of the same.

• • • • • •

Scriptural References

Luke 1:1–4; John 20:30; 2 Timothy 3:16; Hebrews 11

Suggested Additional Sources for Reading

- Marc Zvi Brettler, "Torah: Introduction," in *The Jewish Study Bible* (Oxford Univ. Press, 2004).
- *The Cambridge History of the Bible,* 3 volumes (Cambridge Univ. Press, 1975).
- Lee Martin McDonald, *The Biblical Canon: Its Origin, Transmission, and Authority* (Hendrickson, 2007).
- F. E. Peters, *The Voice, the Word, the Books: The Sacred Scripture of the Jews, Christians, and Muslims* (Princeton Univ. Press, 2007).
- Mark Allen Powell, *Fortress Introduction to the Gospels* (Fortress Press, 1998).

Suggested Questions for Further Discussion/Thought

1. Is there a difference between "truth" and "fact"? Can truth be transmitted through a medium that is not necessarily fact?
2. Read Luke 1:1–4 and John 20:30. Discuss how these passages point to oral traditions that existed before any writing of the gospels occurred.
3. What are your thoughts and feelings about the "infallibility" of the Bible? How have your thoughts about that shifted or stayed the same over time?
4. Do you think that the words that you read in your particular translation are exactly what God said?

How do we reconcile the Old Testament command for vengeance (eye for an eye) with Jesus' command to turn the other cheek and love our enemies?

....

Becky Garrison

Our hatred of the "other" is nothing new. At the time of Jesus' birth, the Samaritans and the Jews had been at each other's throats for literally hundreds of years. At the time when Jesus told the parable of the Good Samaritan (Lk. 10:25–37), the concept of a Samaritan coming to the rescue of a Jew would have been considered just as incongruous as if, say, a Focus on the Family follower marched in the New York City LGBT (Lesbian, Gay, Bisexual, and Transgender) Pride Parade today.

But as the parable made clear, the Samaritan was considered the Jewish man's "neighbor." By implication, that means the definition of "neighbor" has to be expanded to include all of God's children, including those of different social classes, races, creeds, and political affiliations. When Jesus commanded his followers to "go and do likewise" by following the example of the Good Samaritan, he challenged the early church to look beyond its comfort zone. His disciples were required to obey the greatest commandment by showing Jesus' love and kindness to all people because everyone was their "neighbor."

The early Christian church cut across the various hierarchical lines that divided people. It did not seek to dominate the political establishment or maintain the status quo; rather, its goal was to spread the universal love of Christ. In doing that, it transformed the world.

....

Jarrod McKenna

I had just finished running a workshop for Greenpeace, The Wilderness Society, and an antinuclear organization on the history and power of nonviolent direct action in which I had explored and trained people in the transformative nonviolence of Gandhi, Martin Luther King Jr., and to the surprise of many gathered, Jesus. Afterwards a well-respected activist approached me away from others and asked tearfully, "Why was this Jesus not found in my experience of church?"

This question goes to the heart of the gospel, to the heart of mission, and to the heart of discipleship. Why is it that people can't find the hope of the world in our churches? I think it's directly connected to the lack of schooling in letting God's love through us by "loving our enemies"—to be merciful as the triune God is merciful. Fierce Calvary-shaped love is how God has saved us and it's how we are to witness to our salvation. Grace is both how God has saved us and the pattern of kingdom living for which the Holy Spirit empowers us.

"Eye for an eye" is not about vengeance but the limitation of retaliation. In Christ, violence is not only restrained but also transformed. On the cross, God does not overcome evil with evil but with good (Rom. 12:21). There is nothing passive about Jesus' turning the other cheek in the face of injustice (Jn. 18:23). To turn the other cheek is to practice the provocative peace that embodies the healing justice of the kingdom by exposing injustice with the presence of love (Col. 2:15).

We don't need to reconcile vengeance or violence with loving our enemies. Instead, we need to be open to the Holy Spirit's empowerment to witness to God's reconciling the world to Godself through the nonviolent Messiah, Jesus.

••••••••••••••••••••••••••••••••••

Rebecca Bowman Woods

In *Religious Literacy: What Every American Needs to Know and Doesn't,* Stephen Prothero shares the story of a 1995 Colorado murder trial. During deliberations, one juror pulled out his Bible and quoted Leviticus 24, the "eye for an eye" passage that concludes with "He that killeth a man, he shall be put to death." After the juror instructed his fellow jurors to go home and prayerfully consider this passage, they voted unanimously for the death penalty.

The state Supreme Court ordered a new trial, ruling that jurors were not allowed to consult the Bible. Some Christians, led by Colorado-based Focus on the Family, protested the higher court's ruling—perhaps rightly so. Can a court really prevent people of faith from including scripture in their decision making?

But the real injustice, in Prothero's opinion, was that the jurors failed to consider the rest of the Bible, particularly Jesus' views on retaliation in Matthew 5:38–42.

"There are very few passages from the Hebrew Bible that are explicitly refuted in the New Testament, but Leviticus 24:20–21 (echoed in Ex. 21:23–25 and Deut. 19:21) is one of them," writes Prothero, a professor of religious studies at Boston University and a staunch advocate of religious literacy.

Christians should rarely fall back on the argument that the "New Testament supersedes the Old Testament." In Matthew 5, Jesus warns that he has not "come to abolish the law or the prophets" but to fulfill them. He teaches an ethic that "embraces and extends" the law in several instances and refutes it in a few.

Amy Greenbaum, a friend who is in the process of becoming an ordained Reformed rabbi, says the "eye for an eye" text in Leviticus 24 would not have been taken literally, even in ancient times.

....

Kathy Escobar

A. I started seeking God on my own when I was a little girl, apart from my family who were not Christians. I can't explain it, really; I was always drawn to Jesus but couldn't quite make sense of the Old Testament and a lot of the crazy things that were in there—whole communities being wiped out, God's vengeance being poured out left and right. I tried to skip over those parts and somehow erase them from my mind and just focus on Jesus because that was a lot more comforting.

Later, as I began to mature in my faith, I realized I needed to wrestle with this disparity. I admit that I still do. I rest on the new order that Jesus created through the incarnation, turning the old ways upside down. I think the contrast is important; the radical difference between vengeance in the Old and New Testaments makes God's point. Jesus changes everything, teaching what the Kingdom now means.

The Sermon on the Mount clearly sets the stage for this new way that completely demolishes the idea of "an eye for an eye." I don't think I have to pick apart all the reasons why the Old Testament contains certain stories or examples that are utterly confusing and seemingly contrary to God's heart for people. I try to rest on the reality that through the gospels, all that changed. The commands shifted, the law got summed up, and the kingdom principles that Jesus taught were going to be much harder to apply than the old laws by a long shot.

• • • • • •

Scriptural References

Exodus 21:12–26; Leviticus 24:10–23; Matthew 5:3–10, 17–48; 22:37–40, 51; Mark 12:28–31; Luke 6; Romans 5:10, 11; 12

Suggested Additional Sources for Reading

- Dave Andrews, *Plan Be* (published by the author).
- Gregory Boyd, *The Myth of the Christian Religion: Losing your Religion for the Beauty of a Revolution* (Zondervan, 2009).

- Lee C. Camp, *Mere Discipleship: Radical Christianity in a Rebellious World* (Brazos, 2008).

- Becky Garrison, *Red and Blue God, Black and Blue Church* (Jossey-Bass, 2006).

- Kirk Johnson, "Colorado Court Bars Execution Because Jurors Consulted Bible," *The New York Times*, March 29, 2005: http://www.nytimes.com/2005/03/29/national/29bible.html.

- Martin Luther King Jr., *Strength to Love* (Fortress Press, 2010).

- Stephen Prothero, *Religious Literacy: What Every American Needs to Know— and Doesn't* (HarperOne, 2008).

- Stephen Prothero's Web site: http://www.stephenprothero.com.

- Desmond Tutu, *No Future without Forgiveness* (Image, 2000).

- Miroslav Volf, *Exclusion and Embrace* (Abingdon Press, 1996).

- N. T. Wright, *Evil and the Justice of God* (InterVarsity Press, 2009).

Suggested Questions for Further Discussion/Thought

1. What are some of the problems with living out Jesus' "turn the other cheek" ethic?

2. Is killing another human being acceptable for Christians under certain circumstances, or should Christians oppose the death penalty?

3. How is Jesus' summation of the law—"Loving God, loving others as ourselves"—harder than the Old Testament laws?

4. What does it mean that we are called to love as God has loved us?

5. Have you had people ask you why a Jesus who dies for his enemies isn't taught in church?

Is there a right or wrong way to read the Bible?

Jason Boyett

The easiest way to answer that question is to go negative: how not to read the Bible. If you've never read much of the Bible before, don't start on page 1 and try to slog your way through it. The Bible isn't a novel. The beginning, Genesis, is fascinating but you'll lose traction in Leviticus and be completely stuck by the time you get to Numbers.

Don't read the Bible as if it is life's instruction manual. Though it's full of wisdom in books like Proverbs or passages like the Sermon on the Mount, the Bible is not an advice book. Nor is it merely a devotional guide from a single author or a history book about a particular time and place. No, the Bible is a mishmash of literary genres, written across centuries of time by dozens of authors, each with a distinct audience and purpose.

What's the right way to read the Bible? Read it as the revelation of God and God's relationship with his people. It's a messy relationship, colored with sin, failure, sacrifice, salvation, redemption, love, and surprising grace. The Bible has much to say about its own context as well as about our world today, but don't diminish it by thinking of it as a novel, a history book, or an instruction manual. It is those things in part, but on the whole, it is so much more: the great story of God.

Jim L. Robinson

Absolutely. There is a strong tendency to read the scriptures, not in order to hear what the scriptures say (which is the "right" way to read them), but rather to verify what is already believed about the scriptures (which is the wrong way to read them.) The former is called exegesis and latter is called cisegesis.

Joshua Einsohn

Perhaps it's naïve to think that everyone would start reading the Bible with a critical eye, but I believe that all people should read the Bible and try to decide its meaning, as much as they are able, for themselves. Ideally, religious leaders should be there to help facilitate an individual's reading of the Bible, not predigest their flock's faith for them. They should help guide, not impose.

Many people seem to fear what they might discover if they ask too many questions, but the most comfortably faithful folks that I've met have spent a great deal of time rigorously questioning their main religious texts alone or with their friends and their community. The more they struggle with the stories and discover their meanings, the more they find themselves comfortable and secure in their faith.

One of the most interesting Jewish ceremonies I've attended included a "questions from the audience" segment for members of the congregation who had questions about a passage and needed some group debate to help them sort out their thoughts. The people who asked the questions and engaged in debate had clearly spent time thinking on their own before they came in. Their religious leaders and other members in the community helped them to clarify their thinking.

It isn't diminishing one's faith to ask questions about the Bible in order to reach a deeper, more comfortable understanding.

....

José F. Morales Jr.

There are right and wrong ways to read the Bible. I used to move within certain church circles that said there was objective Truth (with a capital "T"). Because of "objective Truth," they argued that logically there could only be one way to read scripture.

I later discovered that the only way was their way, and that their way was laden with a racist and classist agenda: protecting the status quo of the white suburban dominance. Although John 8:32 says the truth will set you free, as a Latino from "da 'hood," there was nothing freeing to me about their readings.

At the other end of the spectrum, postmodernism challenges this idea of objective Truth, and claims at its most extreme that there is no truth. Theologian Catherine Keller, in *On the Mystery* (Fortress Press, 2008), has labeled these two extremes "absolute" and "dissolute." She argues that neither is helpful nor faithful.

I always refer to the story in Luke 10 of the lawyer who asks Jesus, "What must I do to inherit eternal life?" Jesus then answers with a question, "What is written in the law? What do you read there?" The Good News Bible paraphrases the second question: "How do you interpret it?" In other words, what's the right way to read the scriptures? The lawyer answers correctly, "Love God . . . love neighbor." St. Augustine, that great early church father, put it succinctly when he said that any reading of the Bible that gets in the way of loving God and/or neighbor is a wrong interpretation.

We read the Bible to be freed to love, to be empowered to love. To understand what this "love" thing really is, I recommend starting with the Bible.

....

Joshua Toulouse

While there no doubt are traditions that will tell you exactly how the Bible is to be read, the Bible doesn't come with a how-to manual. All anyone can really give you on this question is her or his own opinion, so the easy answer is no, there is no explicitly right or wrong way to read the Bible.

Some people read the Bible to find answers on what exactly they should believe about moral issues, some for inspiration, and others to learn more about where their religion came from or as a guide for where it should be headed. All of these are legitimate ways of reading the Bible, and we all can find ourselves responding to the Bible in any or all of these ways, as well as others, at different points in our lives, and that is completely acceptable.

To get the most out of the Bible, use the many commentaries available to learn more about the historical context that shaped the writing of the books. It is also helpful to recognize that there are different understandings of how various words and phrases should be translated, and that these different translations can dramatically change what meaning we get from the text.

While very few of us have time to learn Hebrew and Greek—the languages in which the Bible was originally written—luckily, there are people who do have time, and we can avail ourselves of their hard work and discover for ourselves which of the many theories we agree with and which theories fit the best with our own theology.

• • • • • •

Scriptural References

Psalm 119:14–16; Luke 24:32; 10:25–37; 1 Corinthians 13:1–2; 2 Timothy 3:16

Suggested Additional Sources for Reading

- Marcus J. Borg, *Reading the Bible again for the First Time: Taking the Bible Seriously but Not Literally* (Harper San Francisco, 2002).

- John A. Buehrens, *Understanding the Bible: An Introduction for Skeptics, Seekers, and Religious Liberals* (Beacon, 2004).

- Bart D. Ehrman, *Jesus, Interrupted: Revealing the Hidden Contradictions in the Bible (and Why We Don't Know about Them)* (HarperOne, 2010).

- Peter J. Gomes, *The Good Book: Reading the Bible with Mind and Heart* (HarperOne, 2002).

- Justo L. González, *Santa Biblia: The Bible through Hispanic Eyes* (Abingdon Press, 1996).
- Alister McGrath, *In the Beginning: The Story of the King James Bible and How It Changed a Nation, a Language, and a Culture* (Anchor, 2002).
- David Plotz, *Good Book: The Bizarre, Hilarious, Disturbing, Marvelous, and Inspiring Things I Learned When I Read Every Single Word of the Bible* (Harper Perennial, 2010).
- *Ryken's Bible Handbook: A Guide to Reading and Studying the Bible* (Tyndale, 2005).
- R. S. Sugirtharajah, ed., *Voices from the Margins: Interpreting the Bible in the Third World* (Orbis Books, 2006).
- N. T. Wright, *The Last Word: Scripture and the Authority of God—Getting beyond the Bible Wars* (HarperOne, 2006).

Suggested Questions for Further Discussion/Thought

1. What kind of risks would be involved if you set aside all preconceived ideas about scripture and approached it as if for the first time?
2. What is "truth"? And how do you know it is truth?
3. Is it wrong to read the Bible with a critical eye? Don't faith leaders do that?
4. Is it possible to come to a different conclusion than your religion does about certain passages without losing your faith or violating the rules of your religion?
5. How should the original context of the various biblical texts shape what they mean to contemporary society?

Does God justify violence in scripture?
What about genocide?

Jarrod McKenna

The Bible doesn't present itself as a collection of refined religious wisdom. The story of God's redemption (the Bible) is as wild, messy and complex as we are. Like Jacob and the angel, what is central to our scriptures is wrestling within the text with God, which climaxes in Christ transfiguring everything through him.

The darkness, horror, and brutality that (miraculously) are not edited out of scripture are nothing other than what God has been wrestling to transform and has done so "in Christ." How our Muslim friends understand their Qur'an is like how we understand the person of Jesus: as the literal Word of God (Jn. 1:14).

If the Bible is authoritative for us (and I hope it is), we must avoid being modern-day Marcionites, editing out (from the Holy Bible or ourselves) that which reveals what God longs to transform. Take the story of genocide in Joshua 11 as an example.

Today, God is no less on the side of oppressed landless minorities fleeing oppressive empires, no less calling us to be a people among them seeking a future of risk against the most powerful military forces in the world, no less a warrior fighting on our behalf. But in Jesus, God has conquered not with a sword, killing his enemies, but with a cross, dying for them (Rev. 12:11). The Bible not only does not justify violence, war, and genocide; in light of Jesus; it abolishes them with the inbreaking of the kingdom.

Brandon Gilvin

The world has always been a violent place. Some of the earliest stories in the Bible acknowledge this. Whether it's the mythic stories from Genesis, such as Cain's murder of Abel, or the later epic stories that recall violence against women, such as the rape of Tamar, violent acts are part of the stories that make up the Bible. The death of Jesus, which serves as the climax of the gospels, is itself an act of state-sponsored violence (seriously . . . how else would you describe capital punishment?).

Different violent acts are treated differently throughout the Bible. Some acts are punished, others are accepted as collateral damage, and some seem sanctioned.

From my perspective, however, those differences have little to do with how God sees violence. Human beings wrote the stories in the Bible and an invisible, divine hand did not direct them. The people of faith that wrote these stories should be understood as fallible human beings who were struggling to make sense of how God was present in their histories. Sometimes they saw God's presence in the violence waged in their history.

Does this mean that we must see violence in biblical stories as divinely inspired? Does it give us permission to excuse our violence as divinely sanctioned?

Modern readings of the stories in Joshua of the violent conquest of Canaan have been used to justify the slaughter of indigenous people in North America, the apartheid-era violence in South Africa, and the ongoing Israeli-Palestinian conflict. Readings of Paul have been used to justify slavery. Prophetic calls for God's punishment of ancient Israel have been used to excuse the Holocaust.

These are abusive readings. It is inexcusable to justify violence with religion. I suggest an alternative way of approaching the Bible—reading it with the knowledge that those who came before us struggled with the way to find God in every detail of their lives and histories and sometimes got it wrong, and remembering that for every act of violence in the Bible, there is a call to justice and peacemaking, and a story about an individual who suffers an act of violence and cries out.

We as the readers are left to choose what we do with that cry. Do we seek vengeance? or work for reconciliation?

....

Gary Peluso-Verdend

One's answer will depend largely on who you think wrote the scriptures. If God is the author and God authorized everything said in God's name, then the answer is yes. However, if you believe human beings authored the scriptures, sometimes inspired by God and sometimes justifying what they wanted to do or had done, then the answer is no. I stand with the latter answer.

There are scores of references to doing violence in God's name, with several justifying reasons. If people are being attacked, they might pray for strength against their enemies (self-defense). When the newly forming people of Israel approached Canaan at the end of their desert wanderings, they began their assaults on the people of the land believing (or writing later to justify their actions) that God had given them the land (conquest). In Elijah's infamous contest with the prophets of Baal, God's prophet exterminated the false prophets (purification), who promoted a polluting religion in the land.

Examples of violence in God's name are evident in the New Testament, too, but the examples differ from the Old Testament period. In the New Testament period, Israel lived as a client state of the Roman Empire and, as such, did not have to wrestle with questions of national defense as it did during the years between David's reign (about 1000 B.C.E.) and the Babylonian captivity (sixth century B.C.E.).

In first-century C.E. Palestine, some Jewish guerilla groups (Zealots) took action into their own hands and struck Roman targets directly. Others prayed and dreamed of the day when Rome would be overthrown and God's reign would be established; this is the theme running through the book of Revelation.

No, God does not justify violence or genocide through the scriptures, but human authors do.

· · · · · ·

Scriptural References

Genesis 6:5–7; 2 Samuel 13; Micah 6:8; Isaiah 11; Joshua 10, 11; 1 Kings 18:20–40; Mark 13; John 1:14; 14:6; Philemon; Hebrews 12:2; Colossians 1:15

Suggested Additional Sources for Reading

- Dave Andrews, *Plan Be* (published by the author).
- Walter Brueggemann, *Divine Presence amid Violence: Contextualizing the Book of Joshua* (Cascade, 2009).
- Lee C. Camp, *Mere Discipleship: Radical Christianity in a Rebellious World* (Brazos, 2008).
- C. S. Cowles, *Show Them No Mercy* (Zondervan, 2003).
- Phyllis Tribble, *Texts of Terror: Literary-Feminist Readings of Biblical Narratives* (Fortress Press, 1984).
- James G. Williams, ed., *The Rene Girard Reader* (Crossroad, 1996).
- Walter Wink, *Engaging the Powers: Discernment and Resistance in an Age of Domination* (Fortress Press, 1992).

Suggested Questions for Further Discussion/Thought

1. How does the violence in the scriptures reveal the violence in ourselves?
2. What would it look like to not "edit out" this violence but let God transform it in Christ?
3. Do you see scriptures still used today to justify violence? How so?
4. How does Jesus' call to nonviolence "perfect" the ancient laws that preceded him?

Hell, Sheol, Hades, Gehenna, and Tartarus are all labeled as "hell" by most Christians. Are they really the same? Are they all places of fiery torment? Are such things to be taken literally, metaphorically, or as myth?

....

David J. Lose

These places aren't all the same, but they're similar enough that you can understand why people lump them together. In brief, "Sheol" and "Hades" represent the realm of the dead, the place where both good and bad people go after death. "Gehenna" and "Tartarus," on the other hand, are reserved for wicked people and are places of punishment. Hell, a word that comes from Old English, has become a catch-all phrase for the others, but for the last two especially.

On the whole, the Bible doesn't talk a whole lot about any of these places and so I'm a little leery of giving them much significance in our own theology. I get downright suspicious of folks that seem to like talking about eternal punishment, as that seems out of sync with Jesus' emphasis on God's love.

Too often in the church's history, hell has been used to scare people into doing what the church wants them to. For this reason, some people think we've outgrown the usefulness of concepts like hell and damnation. Others, however, would argue that we wouldn't appreciate heaven without the threat of hell.

Insofar as hell depicts ultimate separation from God, I tend to think that whether it's an actual physical place or a metaphor, it's a good place to avoid. On that score, I take hope from the apostle Paul's declaration that "neither death, nor life, nor angels, nor rulers, nor things present, nor things to come, nor powers, nor height, nor depth, nor anything else in all creation will be able to separate us from the love of God in Christ Jesus our Lord" (Rom. 8:38–39). Sounds good to me.

Gary Peluso-Verdend

No, the meaning of these words is not the same. Rather, we have different symbols from different symbol systems.

"Sheol" is a Hebrew word, found in the pre-sixth-century-B.C.E. portions of the Old Testament. Ancient Judaism did not conceive of human beings as part body and part soul. Rather, human beings were understood as flesh animated by the breath of God. Whatever existence a person had after death was thought to be in a place called Sheol, a place of shades, where there is no consciousness. Sheol contains neither pleasures nor torments.

During Israel's captivity in Babylon, Jews were exposed to Zoroastrianism, a religion that includes a belief in resurrection and a two-place afterlife—the equivalent of heaven and hell. By New Testament times, belief in resurrection, heaven, and hell were widespread—albeit not universal—in Judaism.

Hell as a place of torment and stink became well developed many centuries after the Bible by the Christian writer Dante Alighieri, but sometimes the roots of a mythical or nonphysical place are found in real places. "Gehenna," as a place of torment for evil people, was associated with the Valley of Hinnom, south of Jerusalem, where the city dumped its garbage.

Very important beliefs are associated with hell, such as sin, judgment, consequence, and resurrection. Christianity—or any other religion—is like a language; one must understand each symbol within a greater grammar.

Jason Boyett

No, they are not the same. Four words—the Hebrew word "Sheol" and the Greek words "Hades," "Gehenna," and "Tartarus"—have been translated as the English word hell. We think of hell as a fiery place of torment for sinners, but only "Gehenna" fits that description.

Sheol was an all-purpose term referring to the shadowy realm of the dead (the grave), and earlier Old Testament books seem to indicate that everyone goes there—not just the wicked. In the New Testament, the Greek word Hades is used interchangeably with Sheol—it's the place of the dead. Tartarus appears only once in the Bible, in 2 Peter 2:4. It refers to Tartarus, the dungeon-like netherworld in Greek mythology filled with suffering and torment. The context indicates it is where demons reside.

The hell-as-torture-chamber idea comes from Gehenna, which Jesus described as a destination for sinners. This word originates with a Hebrew name, Ge-Hinnom, which refers to the Hinnom Valley, a garbage dump outside Jerusalem. Trash, animal carcasses, and the bodies of criminals were dumped there, and the valley burned continuously—an evocative image of hell.

Do we take the idea of a burning hell literally? Jesus certainly spoke as if it were a real place. But keep in mind that the idea of a dualistic afterlife—a hell for sinners and heaven for the righteous—was a relatively new idea to Judaism, possibly due to the influence of Zoroastrianism during the Babylonian exile. It was a theological departure from the ancient faith of the Jewish patriarchs.

....

Craig Detweiler

While death is a certain fact, it is also prompts an air of mystery. What happens when our hearts stop beating? Is there something on the other side of life? Descriptions of hell (and heaven) are all rather speculative, more poetic than precise.

The Hebrew word "Sheol" describes the grave that awaits us all. It is a shadowy place, something we've all glimpsed at a funeral but never experienced from the inside. Our bodies are all bound for Sheol, irrespective of our beliefs or practices. None escape physical death.

When the Hebrew scriptures were translated into the Greek language, the word "Hades" was chosen to describe the ground or pit our bodies are bound for. The Greek notion of Hades was more of a shady, mythological place than a physical grave.

Within Greek mythology, Tartarus is a place of judgment and torment, a pit much farther down than the more benign Hades. Only once does the word Tartarus appear in scripture. In 2 Peter 2:4, God punishes sinful angels by throwing them into Tartarus, a dark pit reserved for judgment.

When the Bible was translated into English, Hades and Sheol were translated as hell. Unfortunately, such a reference comes across as much more loaded than "the grave." It had eternal associations rather than a tangible, temporal, or physical meaning.

The associations of hell with a fire, torment, and eternal anonymity start coming into play with a term like "Gehenna." It is a destination we would all want to avoid. It is a place where people who lack family, resources, and significance are discarded. No one wants to feel so unloved, unacknowledged, or unnoticed.

• • • • • •

Scriptural References

Genesis 37:35; Deuteronomy; 32:22 (Sheol); Psalm 6:5; Romans 8:38–39; Matthew 5:22 (Gehenna) and 16:18 (Hades); 2 Peter 2:4 (Tartarus); 1 John 4:7; Revelation 20:10

Suggested Additional Sources for Reading

- Jason Boyett, *Pocket Guide to the Afterlife* (Jossey-Bass, 2009).
- Stanley N. Gundry et al., *Four Views of Hell* (Zondervan, 1997).
- Alice K. Turner, *The History of Hell* (Mariner, 1995).
- T. J. Wray and Gregory Mobley, *The Birth of Satan: Tracing the Devil's Biblical Roots* (Palgrave Macmillan, 2005).

Suggested Questions for Further Discussion/Thought

1. Why is hell such an important concept to some Christians?
2. What do our beliefs about hell say about our theology, or picture, of God?
3. Most Christians believe in a dualistic afterlife (heaven and hell). Yet a fiery place of torment is in contrast to the idea of Sheol as found in most of the Old Testament. Still, Jesus clearly believes in a fiery hell. Is this a doctrine that "evolved" from the Old Testament to the New Testament? How do you reconcile two contrasting doctrines if both have biblical support?

How can we begin to take the Bible literally when it seems to contradict itself so often?

··
Rebecca Bowman Woods

During my ordination interviews, I was asked my views on the Bible's authorship. My response: While the Bible is sacred scripture, humanity's grubby fingerprints are all over it. Fortunately, the committee liked my answer.

This may seem like a paradox, but for me it's easier to take the Bible seriously by viewing it as a joint venture between God and people rather than picturing God dictating every word and expecting us to read it literally.

Contradictions arise because people wrote it with different theological perspectives across a period of hundreds of years. Some authors tell the same stories again, in different ways. For example, the history of Israel in 1 and 2 Samuel and 1 and 2 Kings is retold in 1 and 2 Chronicles by an author who changed some of the specifics to convey his own views and to answer questions of his own era.

The four gospels tell of Jesus' earthly ministry but the events aren't in the same sequence, and when the gospel writers include the same story, the details are off. And the apostle Paul of the book of Acts is not the same Paul who emerges from reading his letters.

People try to harmonize or overlook these differences, but to the inquisitive reader, they are valuable clues about the authors and their situations. Yes, the biblical authors (and some of the copyists who added to and subtracted from the manuscripts) had agendas, biases, and perspectives, just as all of us do.

Even though biblical stories differ, what the tellers and authors had in common was the experience of God—through personal encounters and the sacred teachings, writings, and traditions of faith communities.

·······························
Gary Peluso-Verdend

Better not to begin to take the Bible literally! Rather, take it seriously and learn to interpret it.

What does it mean to take the Bible literally? Most if not all of the Bible circulated orally at first, sometimes for generations. The transformation from oral to written text occurred in different time periods. By way of various scribes in different places, using varying texts that sometimes contradicted other texts in significant ways, the oral became written.

A variety of literary forms is evident in the Bible: narrative, allegory, parable, poetry, fiction, historical records, reports of fantastical ecstatic experiences, metaphor, and myth (which does not mean "untrue," but is an ahistorical means to express something that is true at the deepest levels). Most of these poetic and literary forms cannot be interpreted literally.

The Bible should be read only in context. The context for reading the Bible will include the historical context and our contemporary context. Responsible readers will seek to be informed by scholarship regarding what the text meant, and they will read the text today with a community of readers that will help keep any reading as honest as possible.

Are there contradictions in the Bible? Yes. Many voices are expressed through the Bible. Think of the Bible as a partial record of the experiences, conversations, and debates of the people of God over time. We are privileged to overhear the conversations and debates embedded in this living document!

It would be a mistake to stifle, repress, or resolve all of the debates and contradictions of contemporary Christianity. Shutting down the debates and resolving the contradictions of the text would diminish the power of the Bible. God speaks with one voice but humankind listens with many ears!

....

Kathy Escobar

When I became a Christian, I immersed myself in the Bible and in extremely conservative evangelical churches that elevated the Bible to the nth degree. I love the Bible. It is a beautiful, challenging, and supernatural book; its words are "sharper than any two-edged sword" (Heb. 4:12).

One thing that has helped me the most over the past years in letting go of Bible worship and assuming that "if you don't take it literally then the whole thing falls apart" is remembering that interpretation of the Bible is varied.

Years ago, a very strict Calvinist friend of mine took a course in biblical counseling. She was dismissing the counseling degree I'd started to pursue at seminary, saying that it was not "biblical enough." I remember heated conversations with her in which I reminded her that her course was merely the instructor's interpretation and application of the Bible. In the same vein, we need to get more honest about that when it comes to literal interpretation.

Each person who "interprets" the Bible can do that work through extensive exegesis, commentaries, and a wide variety of other research, but it is still filtered through that person's lens. It's presumptuous of anyone to think he or she has the market cornered on exactly what God meant. The Bible is just too complicated for that, and there are too many contradictions that can't be completely answered.

As a pastor, I always tell people, "This is just my take on this passage; I am sure there are others who see it differently." I think we need to be more honest about "literal interpretation" and admit that if we really took the Bible literally, most of our churches wouldn't look the way they look, and we wouldn't wear what we wear or care about the things we care about. Many are good at "selective literal interpretation," choosing to align with some passages and completely dismiss others.

I think I am becoming more honest about the inability to reconcile completely the inconsistencies in the Bible. Like so many other issues of faith, intellectualizing them doesn't always work, no matter how hard we try to make sense of it.

....

Joshua Einsohn

A strict, literal interpretation of the Bible is so fraught with potential contradiction that it should be avoided at all costs to prevent either a great deal of teeth gnashing (and expensive dental work) or a slowly numbing lack of critical thought.

In college, I was often in classes with a certain poor girl who was a fundamentalist Christian and believed the literal word of the Bible. Incidentally, I don't consider her to be a "poor girl" because she was a fundamentalist Christian! I felt sorry for her because she kept taking classes that frequently rendered her distraught. Here's how class went pretty much every day for "Jane."

Classmate: If the total population of the world was Adam, Eve, Cain, and
　　　　Abel, and Abel smote Cain and then had the "mark of Cain" put on his
　　　　forehead so that all the rest of the people of the world would know the
　　　　awful thing he did, who are the rest of the people? Mom and Dad?
Jane: (confidently) No, the heathens.
Classmate: It doesn't say anything about God creating heathens.
Jane: (less confidently) Yes it did . . . when he created the beasts.
Classmate: Did you just call all the non-Christians "beasts"?
Jane: (tearing up) Well . . . yes . . .

At this point, the class erupted and she burst into tears. In every class I had with her, the waterworks would start up at least once a week. Her superior critical thinking continually butted up against her literal belief in the Bible. The interesting thing was that she could easily have made it through college without taking those courses, and yet she kept signing up for them. I've always wondered if she managed to reconcile the two sides of herself.

· · · · · ·

Scriptural References

Genesis 1, 2; Matthew 1:18—2:23; 5:21–48; Luke 2:1–20; Hebrews 4

Suggested Additional Sources for Reading

- Karen Armstrong, *The Battle for God* (Ballantine, 2001).
- Marcus J. Borg, *Reading the Bible again for the First Time: Taking the Bible Seriously but Not Literally* (Harper San Francisco, 2002).

Suggested Questions for Further Discussion/Thought

1. Do you think it's possible to take parts of the Bible literally and leave out others?
2. Does fixating on literal interpretation limit God?
3. How are you learning to live with the inconsistencies in the Bible? What does that look like, feel like, for you?
4. Can two statements that seem to contradict each other somehow both be true? If so, how?

Are Lucifer, the Adversary, Satan, the Beast, and the Antichrist all the same? If so, why use so many names? If not, what are their different roles, and who is in charge?

....

David J. Lose

A. The writers of scripture used a number of different names to describe the forces pitted against God's loving and good intentions for creation. The differences reflect the culture, time period, and context of the writers and their communities. "Satan," for instance, derived from Arabic and Persian words among the cultures surrounding Israel, means "the adversary," and is used to describe various beings that sometimes tempt, sometimes test, and sometimes torment human beings.

While each of these names may have had specific meaning for the communities for which various books of the Bible were written, in our own time the terms have often been lumped together, and what we "know" about them comes more from extrabiblical sources ranging from Jewish and Christian folklore to Dante's *Inferno* and the more recent Left Behind series.

While there may be some small comfort found in recognizing that there is no single and all-powerful demonic being waiting to jump out at us, we shouldn't kid ourselves: The biblical authors are keenly aware of the strong impulse to sunder our relationship with God, creation, and each other, and the devastating consequences of giving in to that impulse. Little wonder that the Apostle Paul says "the whole creation" groans in anticipation of the redemption and victory over evil that Christ's return represents.

In light of this, Christians can both set themselves against any and all forces that run contrary to God's goodwill for creation—whatever name or guise those forces might take—and faithfully keep on their lips the prayer that closes Revelation: "Come, Lord Jesus!" (Rev. 22:20).

....

Jason Boyett

A. No, they're not the same, though in today's religious culture you'd be forgiven for thinking they were just different names for the primary enemy of God.

The "adversary" is an English translation of *ha-satan*, a Hebrew word describing the biblical entity who seems to act as a prosecutor in God's court (see Zech. 3:1–7). In New Testament writings, however, this adversary evolves into Satan or the devil, God's primary opposition.

"Lucifer" is a name derived from the Latin translation of Isaiah 14:12, a prophecy about a mysterious Babylonian king—the "morning star" (lucerne ferre) who has been cast down to earth. Along with Ezekiel 28, medieval theologians reinterpreted this passage as a reference to Satan, and the name stuck.

In Revelation, "the Beast" is used to describe the falsely messianic world leader who does Satan's bidding in the final battle between God and evil. We know of this leader as "the Antichrist," though that name doesn't actually appear in Revelation.

So in summary, "Lucifer" is a misnomer and probably shouldn't be part of the discussion. "The Beast" and/or "the Antichrist" are names for a man. "The Adversary" (*ha-satan*) in the Old Testament is a member of the heavenly council under God's control, and the New Testament Satan is the archenemy of the Almighty.

If anyone's "in charge," I guess it would be Satan, the New Testament one (sigh).

• • • • • •

Scriptural References

Isaiah 14:12; Zechariah 3:1–7; Matthew 25:41; Revelation 19:20

Suggested Additional Sources for Reading

- Gerald Massadie, *A History of the Devil* (Kodansha Globe, 1997).

- Elaine Pagels, *The Origin of Satan: How Christians Demonized Jews, Pagans, and Heretics* (Vintage, 1996).

- T. J. Wray and Gregory Mobley, *The Birth of Satan: Tracing the Devil's Biblical Roots* (Palgrave Macmillan, 2005).

Suggested Questions for Further Discussion/Thought

1. How many of our ideas about the devil, hell, and so on do you think you can actually trace back to the Bible? What are some of the other sources that have influenced our thinking on these matters?

2. While the specific character of Satan may be unclear based on the Bible, it is clear that he is seen as a source of evil. Why is it important, in a monotheistic religion, for someone or something to be responsible for the world's evil?

3. If you believe in an entity or spirit such as Satan in the universe, what sort of agency or power does it have over our world and lives?

Was Mary Magdalene a prostitute?

· · · · · · · · · · · · · · · · · · · ·

Becky Garrison

Even though Mary had the courage to go inside and proclaim the
good news that "I have seen the Lord," (Jn. 20:18), the church couldn't
handle the truth that a woman delivered the news that changed the world.
So church tradition pegged her as the penitent sinner (read "prostitute").
By some accounts, she's the woman caught in adultery who is about to
be stoned before Jesus saved her (Jn. 7:53–8:11) or the sinful woman who
anointed Jesus' feet with perfume and her tears (Lk. 7:36–50).

But if this was case, then why is she not identified by name in these
instances, yet she's referenced elsewhere in the Bible? Yes, Luke reports that
she had seven demons come out of her but he's silent on the nature of her
disease (Lk. 8:1–3).

Given that history seems to have been written by the winners, the
church tends to focus on the male disciples. As we know, they ran for the
hills. All too often, church historians neglect to focus on those women who
not only stayed with Christ until the end but also assisted in the burial of the
only man who truly embraced them as equals in the kingdom of God. Even
the disciples dismissed these firsthand accounts as nonsense, demonstrating
the lack of respect accorded to women in first century Judea (Lk. 24:11).

And while we're at it, let's put an end to this gnostic nonsense that she
was married to Jesus. Since when did *The Last Temptation of Christ* and *The Da
Vinci Code* become part of the biblical canon?

· · · · · · · · · · · · · · · · · ·

Marcia Ford

Probably the most accurate answer to that is that we don't know
for sure. However, the contemporary consensus is that she was not
a prostitute and that her reputation as such resulted from a sixth-century
sermon by Pope Gregory the Great, who misinterpreted several Bible
passages. Efforts to correct that have intensified in recent decades, both in
the Roman Catholic Church, where the error had long been kept alive, and
among Protestants, who often didn't know what to make of her.

This is what we know: Mary was from the town of Magdala near the Sea
of Galilee. Jesus cast out seven demons from her. She began following him

and has the distinction of being mentioned in the Bible more often than some of the twelve disciples.

Here's what is questionable: Some believe Mary Magdalene was the "sinful" woman who washed Jesus' feet with her tears, wiped them with her hair, kissed them, and poured perfume on them (Lk. 7:37–50), but the Bible never identifies the woman by name. Immediately after this passage, Luke mentions Mary Magdalene (Lk. 8:2), but he mentions several other women as well and doesn't make a connection with the earlier passage.

Adding to the confusion have been artistic and popular representations of Mary Magdalene as a prostitute, such as Jean Beraud's 1891 painting, *Mary Magdalene in the House of Simon the Pharisee,* the 1970 rock opera (and subsequent movie) *Jesus Christ Superstar,* and Mel Gibson's 2004 film *The Passion of the Christ.*

....

Brandon Gilvin

There is absolutely no evidence that Mary Magdalene—more properly referred to as Mary of Magdala—was a prostitute. It's an old tradition that has been used for sexist ends but has no real biblical basis.

The persistent claim that Mary Magdalene was a prostitute is rooted in a couple of things. There are seven women named Mary in the New Testament. These include the following:

- Jesus' mother Mary
- Mary Magdalene (Mary of Magdala)
- The Mary with a sister named Martha in Luke 10
- Mary, the wife of Clopas, in John 19
- Mary, the mother of James and Joseph, witness of the Resurrection at the ends of Matthew, Mark, and Luke
- Mary, the mother of John Mark, in Acts 12
- The Mary that Paul refers to in Romans 16

Many traditions have amalgamated some of these Marys, especially Mary Magdalene and Mary, the sister of Martha. It is possible that they are the same person, but we have no way of proving that, one way or the other.

At some point, the church began to assume that a woman referred to as "sinful" who anointed Jesus in Luke 7 was Mary Magdalene. Luke's gospel does not identify this woman as Mary Magdalene (though in a similar story in John, Mary, sister of Martha anoints Jesus, but she is not referred to as "sinful"), nor does it describe the woman's sinfulness as sexual in any way. However, if you are at all familiar with this story, you probably imagine Mary Magdalene, former prostitute, crying and anointing because Jesus has forgiven her.

For that, you can thank Pope Gregory the Great. In 591 C.E., he delivered a sermon in which he combined these many Marys with the woman of Luke 7, and though the text intimates nothing, he contended that she was a prostitute.

Mary was one of many women who were part of the early Jesus movement, perhaps even on par with Peter as an early leader. Mary also may have been a woman of means, as Luke 8 says that the women supported the disciples financially. John also contends that she had an extended conversation with the resurrected Christ.

....

Jim L. Robinson

The idea that Mary was a prostitute is an example of a need some people feel to decorate and embellish the scriptures, perhaps to make them more interesting and appealing. The same license is taken in regard to the Samaritan woman who met Jesus at Jacob's well near the village of Sychar (Jn. 4).

Fred Craddock recalls hearing a sermon in which the preacher said of the woman of Sychar, "She was wearing a short skirt, slit up the side. She wore fishnet stockings and her feet were pushed into spike heels. Her sweater was two sizes too small, and she was leaning on a lamp post, smoking a cigarette in a long holder."

Fred says, "I don't know where he got all that; but I was thirteen, and I was interested!"

Interested, but misled. I wonder how many ideas are floating around in the church whose origin is in that kind of embellishment of the scriptures! All the more reason to read and reread the scriptures for yourself!

• • • • • •

Scriptural References

Matthew 27:56, 61; 28:1; Mark 15:40, 47; 16:1, 9; Luke 7:36–50; 8:1–3; 24:10–11; John 7:53—8:11; 20:1–2, 11–18; 19:25

Suggested Additional Sources for Reading

- Christians for Biblical Equality: http://www.cbeinternational.org.

- Bart D. Ehrman, *Peter, Paul, and Mary Magdalene: The Followers of Jesus in History and Legend* (Oxford Univ. Press, 2008).

- Elisabeth Schüssler Fiorenza, *In Memory of Her* (Crossroad, 1994).

- Margaret George, *Mary, Called Magdalene* (Penguin, 2003).
- Liz Curtis Higgs, *Unveiling Mary Magdalene: Discover the Truth about a Not-So-Bad Girl of the Bible* (WaterBrook, 2004).
- Karen King, *The Gospel of Mary Magdala* (Polebridge, 2003).
- "Scholars seek to correct Christian tradition, fiction of Mary Magdalene": http://www.catholic.org/national/national_story.php?id=19680.
- Amy Welborn, *De-Coding Mary Magdalene: Truth, Legend, and Lies* (Our Sunday Visitor, 2006).

Suggested Questions for Further Discussion/Thought

1. Why have artists been so fascinated with Mary Magdalene as an ex-prostitute? What does it say about our culture that this mischaracterization—that of the repentant sexual sinner—makes her so fascinating?

2. Can you remember some Bible stories from childhood? Were they embellished by curriculum or feltboard stories in Sunday school or Vacation Bible School?

3. *The Da Vinci Code* and other books, movies, and Web sites have prompted a great deal of interest in Mary Magdalene. How have such theories affected your faith or your perspective on Jesus' humanity?

4. Can you see any parallels between the portrayals of Mary Magdalene in contemporary society, particularly in the church, and the way that female leaders are portrayed?

Are there any mistakes in the Bible? Like what?

· · · · · · · · · · · · · · · · · ·
David J. Lose

That depends upon what you mean. If by "mistake" you mean that biblical authors wrote something they didn't intend, then no. But if you mean that there are things in the Bible that aren't factually accurate, then the answer is yes.

Before getting too upset by this, it's important to keep in mind that factual accuracy, as we understand it today, is a relatively modern invention. Prior to the Enlightenment and the rise of a scientific worldview, people didn't think in terms of facts that could be verified but rather in terms of truth that could be believed.

Nowhere in its pages does the Bible claim to be a science or history textbook. Rather, it is a collection of the confessions of Israel and the early church about what God was up to in the world. Near the end of his gospel, John doesn't say he wrote "in order to prove beyond a shadow of a doubt that Jesus is the messiah." Instead he writes, "so that you may believe . . ." (Jn. 20:30–31).

The question to ask, then, when one encounters an apparent mistake is not, "Is this accurate?" but rather, "What is the author trying to confess about God?"

For instance, Matthew, Mark, and Luke all say that Jesus was crucified on the Passover. John, however, says it was the day before the Passover. Did John make a mistake? No, he was making a confession that Jesus is the Passover lamb who takes away the sin of the world, and so in his account Jesus dies the evening before Passover, at the exact time the Passover lambs were slaughtered. John didn't make a mistake; he made a confession of faith.

· ·
Rebecca Bowman Woods

The biblical text has a long and sometimes controversial history. Original manuscripts were copied and recopied over centuries. According to scholar and author Bart Ehrman, in his book *Misquoting Jesus*, there are more than fifty-seven hundred Greek manuscripts of the New Testament alone. So it's no surprise that errors were introduced. And that's before the texts were translated into Latin, and later, the King's English.

On top of errors introduced in the process of reproducing and translating, some copyists made editorial changes—adding their own interpretations and embellishments, and deleting or changing passages to make the text more socially acceptable.

For example, check out Romans 16:7. Does your Bible read "Greet Andronicus and Junias," or "Greet Andronicus and Junia"? It's not simply a letter being added or subtracted. Junia was a common Latin name for women; Junias is assumed to be a man's name, but there are no instances of this name in ancient literature.[2] Why does it matter? Because Junia is the only female apostle mentioned in the New Testament. Erasing her, and the scriptural argument that women were apostles, was as simple as adding a letter.

All of this can hardly be reassuring to anyone who wants to read and interpret the Bible with confidence and use it as a basis for living. I recommend buying a good study Bible, translated and compiled by a panel of scholars (not just one or two). Study Bibles have footnotes explaining where variations in the text are significant. Of course, this doesn't mean you can't enjoy reading *The Message* or the traditional *King James Version,* or other paraphrases or translations.

· · · · · · · · · · · · · · · · · · ·

Jason Boyett

Some Christians believe that because the Bible was inspired by God, it cannot contain mistakes or contradictions. Why? Because God is perfect, and something God "wrote" must be perfect. But, inspiration aside, we should remember that scripture was written by men over centuries, during a primitive time. It seems logical that some passages may not agree with each other.

Some mistakes can be explained based on the primitive science of the time—for example, biblical writers thought the sun revolved around the earth. Today we know better. But other mistakes are due to factual inconsistencies from one passage to another. A famous one is the account of the "Cleansing of the Temple."

Matthew, Mark, and Luke report that this event occurred in the week before Jesus was crucified, at the end of his ministry (Mt. 21:12–13). But in John, this event takes place at the beginning of Jesus' ministry (Jn. 2:12–25). The rational explanation is that John got the chronology wrong, or altered the timeline for theological/literary reasons. But biblical literalists, attempting to prove the Bible is without error, explain the contradiction by saying Jesus cleansed the temple twice—once at the beginning of his ministry and then again at the end.

Remember that the gospel accounts were written decades after the time of Christ and passed along largely via storytelling. It seems reasonable that some of the details among different accounts wouldn't match up exactly. Less reasonable are the interpretive gymnastics required to harmonize these contradictions in the name of "perfection."

....

Jim L. Robinson

A. Bottom line: We are not justified on the basis of the accuracy of our biblical interpretations. We are justified by trusting in the grace of God. In my own observation, when this question comes up the one defending the scripture is virtually always really defending himself. (e.g., I believe in grace; but just in case, I want to make sure that I'm 100 percent correct in my understanding of doctrine.) The nagging question of assurance is always taunting; what if you're wrong?

The Bible is not a "fact sheet" about God. It is a witness to human experiences of the presence and action of God. God interacts with people, those people recognize and understand (being inspired) the meaning or purpose of that presence and action, and then they record the experience. In the past, some of those records were collected and became accepted as "scripture"—the Bible. Those kinds of experiences—and the record of the same—continue today.

For the most part, scripture emerged out of Eastern worldviews, whereas we in North America are the products of Greek, or Western, worldviews. The question of "mistakes" imposes a Western worldview onto a basically Eastern document, and is, indeed, irrelevant insofar as it relates to experience. Any perceived contradiction within scripture, or between scripture and experience, is more a measure of our preconceived, often errant, assumptions (based on Western logic) than of the content or intent of scripture.

• • • • • •

Scriptural References

Matthew 28; Mark 16; Luke 24; John 20 (four resurrection accounts); Matthew 26:17–19; Mark 14:12–16; Luke 22:7–13; John 19:31; 20:30–31; Romans 16:7

Suggested Additional Sources for Reading

- Michael Joseph Brown, *What They Don't Tell You: A Survivor's Guide to Biblical Studies* (Westminster John Knox Press, 2000).

- Bart D. Ehrman, *Jesus, Interrupted: Revealing the Hidden Contradictions in the Bible (and Why We Don't Know about Them)* (HarperOne, 2010).

- Bart D. Ehrman, *Misquoting Jesus: The Story behind Who Changed the Bible and Why* (HarperOne, 2007).
- David J. Lose, *Making Sense of Scripture: Big Questions about the Book of Faith* (Fortress Press, 2009).
- Luther Seminary: http://www.EntertheBible.org.
- *The New Interpreter's Study Bible: New Revised Standard Version with Apocrypha* (Abingdon Press, 2003).
- Heidi Bright Parales, *Hidden Voices: Biblical Women and Our Christian Heritage* (Smyth & Helwys, 1998).

Suggested Questions for Further Discussion/Thought

1. Is there a difference between "truth" and "fact"? Can parts of the Bible be "true" whether they are "fact" or not?
2. Why do you think it is so important for some Christians to try to prove that the Bible is factually accurate about everything?
3. To what extent is your faith based on the factual accuracy of the Bible as opposed to the message of the Bible?
4. To the extent that faith relies on the scripture, how do we deal with the fact that the Bible we use may not say exactly what was said or written centuries ago?
5. Do you believe that the errors and changes to the Bible can be explained by saying they are part of God's plan? Why or why not?

In some cases, Paul (the purported author of many New Testament books) seems to support women in leadership roles in church, and in others, he says they have no place. Which is it? And why the seeming contradiction?

....

Becky Garrison

A. Paul's demonstrated support of Lydia, Phoebe, Prisca (Priscilla), and Chloe illuminates the pivotal role that women played in those early churches formed after Pentecost (see Acts 16:40; Rom. 16:1–16 and 1 Cor. 1:11). His other references to women in ministry need to be assessed against the sociopolitical background of Greco-Roman culture.

A commandment such as the requirement that women should cover their heads (1 Cor. 11:3–16) encourages women to follow societal norms. A woman with an uncovered head would draw undue attention to the followers of a religion that was being persecuted by the Roman Empire. Hence, Paul is addressing a specific congregational concern instead of making global pronouncements that are applicable to the entire body of Christ.

Also, one must look at the authenticity of these letters. Romans, 1 and 2 Corinthians, Galatians, Philippians, 1 Thessalonians, and Philemon are seen as "undisputed," meaning there's a consensus among scholars that they can be attributed to Paul. A letter such as Ephesians, which requires women to submit to their husbands (Eph. 5:22–33), is a letter that some scholars believe was either written or edited at a later date.

As the church became more closely aligned with empire, it began to tone down some of its more radical teachings, such as the full equality of all in Christ.

....

David J. Lose

A. Keep in mind two things when reading Paul. First, he's a missionary, not a systematic theologian. Second, Paul anticipates Jesus' imminent return, so his top priority is sharing the good news with as many people as possible.

Today, we tend to read Paul as though he set out to write a timeless theological treatise when he was, instead, providing pastoral responses to particular and often complicated circumstances. This means that we may read as universal and eternal those ethical and theological instructions that Paul intended as particular and provisional.

As far as we can tell, Paul assumed and welcomed women leaders in ministry. Consider, for instance, the baptismal formula he repeats to the Galatians (and the departure from traditional gender hierarchies of the day it represents): "As many of you as were baptized into Christ have clothed yourselves with Christ. There is no longer Jew or Greek, there is no longer slave or free, there is no longer male and female; for all of you are one in Christ Jesus" (Gal. 3:27–28). Keep in mind, also, that Paul names one of his female companions, Junia, as an apostle (Rom. 16:7).

At the same time, if Paul was concerned that this change in social patterns would prove an impediment to the spread of the gospel in a community like Corinth, he would counsel that women keep their heads veiled as a sign of their continued secondary status until full liberation when Christ (soon!) came again (1 Cor. 11:2–16).

After Paul's time, there was a split among early Christians regarding gender equality. The author of the Letter to Timothy (attributed to Paul—in the ancient world, it was not uncommon to write in the name of one's teacher) constrains that equality, a view that eventually became normative in the early church.

....

Joshua Toulouse

Throughout Paul's writings, there are many references to women as leaders in the church and as ideal role models for Christians to follow. There are also a couple of verses attributed to Paul that are not at all supportive of women's roles in the church.

The problematic verses are 1 Corinthians 14:34–36 and 1 Timothy 2:12, 15. Most scholars do not believe that 1 and 2 Timothy are actually written by Paul. These verses state that a woman shouldn't be allowed to teach. No one doubts that Paul wrote 1 Corinthians, however, so the verse that states that women should be silent in church and that it is shameful for them to speak is still problematic. It's also very contradictory to the many times when Paul mentions women leaders in an affirming way.

While it is agreed that the letter to Corinth was written by Paul, it is now believed that this section was a later addition. First, it contradicts an earlier section of the letter (1 Cor. 11:5, 13) that acknowledges that women do pray and prophesy. Also, this section seems to disrupt the sequence in 14:31–33, 37–40; while those are about prophets and prophesy, 34–36 seems completely out of place.

Finally, these sections are not present in all manuscripts of this letter. It is likely that Paul did not write these verses against women, since there are many more instances of scripture in which Paul speaks about women leaders.

·························

José F. Morales Jr.

First things first: The Bible was written by men reared in a strongly patriarchal society. Therefore, we should read scripture with what feminists call "a hermeneutic of suspicion," weeding out the dangerous patriarchal elements.

With this said, Paul, of all people, was a powerful witness for equality. When Paul declares that there is therefore "no longer male or female" (Gal. 3:26–28), he became the first in antiquity to pronounce equality. Moreover, Paul worked with women and called them "prophets," "deacons," and "apostles." Paul considered Junia "prominent among the apostles" (Rom. 16:7). He also mentioned Priscilla before her husband Aquila (Rom. 16:3), which is significant. Paul affirms female leadership.

Having said this, there are antiwomen texts included in scripture, but so are all those passages that affirm female leadership. So we ultimately make a choice. In *The Good Book,* Peter Gomes separates biblical practice from biblical principle, noting that even though a couple of texts speak to the contrary, the early church overwhelmingly practiced inclusion, making the early Christian gatherings "the most egalitarian groups of their day" (Wills, *What Paul Meant,* 90).

In this case, I think the church should preach what it practices.

·····························

Gary Peluso-Verdend

Let's address the last question first. Contradictions may occur because an author changed his mind over time. Or there may be contradictory stances in one book of the Bible because we are reading two different authors, made less visible to us now by an editor who merged two voices into one biblical book.

When it comes to the role of women in the church, the scholars I follow believe we are reading the latter situation. Some scholars argue that Paul's radical views on the equality of women and men in the church and in Christ led the persons who edited his letters to shave the edges off his radical stance.

In many gospel stories and in what scholars accept as the authentic writings of Paul, women are accorded equality with men. Paul's statement in

Galatians 3:28 is foundational: ". . . there is no longer male or female; for all of you are one in Christ Jesus."

Contemporary scholars make strong arguments that this text, and other writings that indicate women in leadership roles—the evangelist/teacher Prisca, the female in a male–female traveling couple in the early church (also Phoebe in Rom. 16:1–2, where she is given the same leadership title as men have)—describe the roles women were accorded. Many scholars take writings such as "Women keep silence in the churches" as pushback forces by later editors rather than as authentic expressions of Jesus' way.

The Bible does not express only one voice. Rather, the Bible is a living book expressing conversations and arguments both within particular communities and over time between communities. It is our privilege to be able to join the conversations and the arguments.

· · · · · ·

Scriptural References

Romans 16:1–2, 3–7, 12; 1 Corinthians 11:5, 13; 14:31–40; Galatians 3:28; Philippians 4:2–3; 1 Timothy 2:12, 15

Suggested Additional Sources for Reading

- Christians for Biblical Equality: http://www.cbeinternational.org.
- Elisabeth Schüssler Fiorenza, *Bread Not Stone: The Challenge of Feminist Biblical Interpretation* (Beacon, 1995).
- Peter J. Gomes, *The Good Book: Reading the Bible with Mind and Heart* (HarperOne, 2002), especially chap. 7, "The Bible and Women: The Conflicts of Inclusion."
- Amy-Jill Levine, with Marianne Blickenstaff, eds., *A Feminist Companion to Paul* (T & T Clark, 2004).
- Alister McGrath, *Heresy: A History of Defending the Truth* (HarperOne, 2009).
- Carol A. Newsom and Sharon H. Ringe, *The Women's Bible Commentary* (Westminster John Knox Press, 1998).
- John Reumann, *Ministries Examined: Laity, Clergy, Women, and Bishops in a Time of Change* (Fortress Press, 1987).
- Krister Stendahl, *The Bible and the Role of Women: A Case Study in Hermeneutics* (Fortress Press, 1973).
- Phyllis Tribble, *Texts of Terror: Literary-Feminist Readings of Biblical Narratives* (Fortress Press, 1984).
- Gary Wills, *What Paul Meant* (Penguin, 2007), especially chap. 5, "Paul and Women."

Suggested Questions for Further Discussion/Thought

1. Ultimately, does the Bible support or disallow female leadership? How do you make your case for or against it?

2. Would learning that many scholars believe that 1 Timothy and 1 Corinthians 14:34–36 were not written by Paul change the way you see them as "scripture"?

3. What would the apostle Paul say to female leaders in the church today?

4. What do you think Paul's reaction would be to those churches who do not allow women to serve in leadership positions equal to men?

Are some sins worse or better than others?

Nadia Bolz-Weber

A. It's important to recognize the difference between "big-S Sin" and "little-s sins." Big-S sin is the human state of being "turned in on self" without a thought of God or neighbor. Big-S sin is putting ourselves on God's throne and not allowing God to be God for us. The fancy Latin that Martin Luther used was *se encurvatus en se*: the self turned in on the self. This phrase describes that state of big-S sin in which every human being on the planet lives.

Little-s sins are the result of big-S sin. However, even if someone managed to pull off not committing little-s sin, he or she would still be plagued with big-S Sin. Yet part of Christianity tries to come off as a way to avoid little-s sin so that you are progressively sanctified until—poof—you are without big-S sin.

For the record, Lutherans like myself do not think this is actually possible, even though it sounds really nice.

Now, back to the question. Are some little-s sins worse than others? Yes. Are some little-s sins better than others? No. (Leave it to a Lutheran to make something a paradox.) But here's the thing: The sin of murder is more harmful than the sin of, say, stealing a saltshaker from Denny's. But the big-S Sin of the sinner who stole the saltshaker is no less than the big-S Sin of the sinner who killed another sinner.

Being Christian does not mean that we follow a really great Sin Management Program. It means that we confess that the grace of God is sufficient.

> [I]f grace is true, you must bear a true and not a fictitious sin. God does not save people who are only fictitious sinners. Be a sinner and sin boldly, but believe and rejoice in Christ even more boldly. For he is victorious over sin, death, and the world.[1] —Martin Luther

---

1. Letters I, *Luther's Works*, American ed. (Fortress, 1963), 48:281–82.

Gary Peluso-Verdend

A. Yes, but first let's define sin. In the United States, we tend to think of "sin" and "sex" together. That pairing is most unfortunate, for both a healthy understanding of sex as well as a healthy understanding of sin. This limitation of "sin" to "sex" and, secondarily, to some vices (e.g., gambling, drinking, or smoking) leads us Christians to overattend to sexual sin and underattend to other areas of sin. For example, in a recent national election, most Americans polled did not understand war as a moral issue.

Sin is a condition of broken relationship, the act of breaking a relationship, living in broken relationships, and acting in ways that would perpetuate a broken relationship. By this definition, murder is sin, insulting a colleague is sin, and passing laws that perpetuate injustice is sin. I've heard some interpreters quote Paul to the effect that, since "all have sinned and fallen short of the glory of God," all sin is equal. Paul's statement might be correctly used to argue that all human beings are sinners, but not that all sins are equally weighty. Catholic moral theology has long argued that some sins were more (mortal) or less (venial) severe.

Certainly, murder is a worse sin than stealing a piece of candy. Abusing a child is a worse sin than flipping off the driver who cut you off in traffic.

Consider this principle: The more people are affected, the more permanent are the negative consequences, the deeper and broader and more irreparable the broken relationships, the worse the sin.

Joshua Einsohn

A. Well, some sins are a lot more fun than others! (Rim shot, please!)

I'm not really one to worry about the afterlife. If there is one, I think everyone pretty much has it wrong. A favorable judgment isn't going to come from specifically taking, say, Jesus into your heart. Taking love into your heart, sure. But all the exclusionary rules that fall under the category of "sin" are far too inconsistent to be what actually happens.

I have to believe that the sin of stealing your stapler from work isn't going to compete with the sin of hypocrisy. I have to believe that the people who claim to do God's work by making miserable the lives of those who are different from them aren't really allowed a free pass when it comes to cleansing their conscience.

Even within the Ten Commandments, some are quite obviously good guidelines but some are a little hazy. Don't kill anyone. Don't take what's not yours. Don't lie. Stop checkin' out your neighbor's firm butt because you might try to do something about it.

Solid advice. Telling your buddy that the hideous item of clothing that he's fallen in love with looks good on him . . . well, yes that may be bearing false witness, but it comes from a good place, so that's gotta be OK, right?

The whole "sin" thing seems to be on a sliding scale to me, but I've always operated under the idea that all sins are not created equally and that the best we can do is to avoid the big ones and try to learn not to commit the smaller ones . . . often.

· · · · · ·

Scriptural References

Exodus 20; 21:23–25; Matthew 23:23–24; Romans 3:9–18; 6:1–13

Suggested Additional Sources for Reading

- Sallie McFague, *Models of God* (Fortress Press, 1987).
- Reinhold Niebuhr, *Moral Man and Immoral Society* (Charles Scribner's Sons, 1932).
- Steven Paulson, *Luther for Armchair Theologians* (Westminster John Knox Press, 2004).
- Paul Tillich, *Shaking the Foundations* (Charles Scribner's Sons, 1940).

Suggested Questions for Further Discussion/Thought

1. What is the punishment for a sin? Does punishment vary by sin?
2. Can you truly cleanse yourself of a sin? If so, how? (i.e., confession, Hail Mary, asking forgiveness on Yom Kippur, etc.)
3. What is the difference between being in a state of Sin and committing sin?
4. Do you believe in original sin (the idea that all humans live in sin because Adam and Eve were sinful)? Why or why not?

If people have to be Christians to go to heaven, what happens to all of the people born before Jesus or who never hear about his ministry?

....

David J. Lose

A. There are different ways of answering this question. Some who are very strict on such matters would say that people who are born before Jesus or never heard of him are just plain out of luck. Others, drawing on a phrase from the Apostle's Creed—"he descended to the dead"—say that between his crucifixion and resurrection, Jesus actually went to the land of the dead to encounter those born before him to give them a chance to believe. (Some early Christian art powerfully depicts Jesus pulling Adam and Eve out of hell.) Still others would say that everyone will ultimately stand before the judgment seat of God and at that time will have the chance to confess Jesus.

Me? I think that it's pretty hard to know for sure and probably comes down to a matter of trust. That is, my question would be: Do we trust the God who has been so merciful and loving to us to take care of people who were born before Jesus or haven't heard of him? I, for one, do.

So maybe, in the end, it's not the best question for us to ask. I mean, rather than worrying about all the people who never had a chance to hear about Jesus, maybe we should instead just get out there and tell people about him—not so much from some fear of people not getting into heaven but rather from a sense of wanting to share the joy, love, and courage we have in Christ.

....

Jarrod McKenna

A. On that day, all who have died were raised from the dead as all of creation gathered around the glory of his burning throne. As the brilliance of the seraphim and cherubim circled above, humanity was separated into two groups. Some started asking each other, "Did you accept Jesus?" In both groups, you could hear people saying,

I went forward at that rally!
I've never heard of Jesus!
I went to church and played in the band!
I was born centuries before him!

I drove out demons and did deeds of power in his name!
I hope I get to go to heaven!

The Son of Man, frustrated with the talk of "going to heaven," interrupted the "babel" and confusion with a clarifying question that silenced all of creation: "You thought this was about going somewhere else? Did I teach you to pray 'Your kingdom we'll go?' or 'Your kingdom come?' I have come to bring heaven here, not to take you elsewhere. Heaven isn't a 'place' that you go; it's the very presence of God that I bring. And now, those who have responded to God's grace and have not dammed heaven from flooding the earth by accepting me will inherit this kingdom of a transformed creation."

The oceans roared with the outcry and joy from within both groups, as some lamented that they had never heard of Jesus, let alone accepted him, while others were so ecstatic that they prophesied and saved souls in his name.

Then the Son of Man, with a voice like lightening, silenced both groups with this stunning declaration: "You accepted me—as a child starving in Darfur, as a refugee seeking to enter your country, as a disabled black youth on death row, as a homeless vet on the streets, as a drug-addicted prostitute needing a meal, as an inmate needing a visit . . ."

As the list went on, and on, a wave of shock rippled throughout all of creation at the realization that the two groups were not separated by their beliefs about Jesus, or grace, or heaven, but by the response to the grace of Jesus among the most vulnerable and oppressed. The reality of this for one group felt like eternal punishment. And for the other, eternal life.

....

Jim L. Robinson

Concerning those born before Jesus, the common evangelical response emerges out of the New Testament epistle to the Hebrews. Chapter 11 is frequently called the "faith chapter." In that chapter, there is a roll call of heroes of the faith, and in each case the text says they lived in faith. They trusted that God would act to save God's people.

The New Testament is offered as the account of the fulfillment of that anticipated saving action of God.

In an overly simplistic way, those who lived prior to Christ were saved because they trusted the promise, and those who live after Christ are saved when they trust that Christ was, indeed the fulfillment of God's promise.

People do not "go to heaven" because they are "Christians." They "go to heaven" because they trust some manifestation of God's grace. While I do not experience the presence and grace of God except through my faith in

Jesus, there are hints in Jesus' own teachings (e.g., Jn. 10:16 and others) that God is reaching out in other ways, too.

Paul and Barnabas in Lystra preached to people who had never heard of God or Jesus and said to them, "God has not left himself without witness." The idea was that God has made God's presence and grace manifest in every time and in every culture. People who trust God on the basis of any of those manifestations seem to me to be "covered."

● ● ● ● ● ●

Scriptural References

Matthew 5:9–13; 7:21–23; 25:31–46; Romans 8:38–39; Ephesians 2:8–10

Suggested Additional Sources for Reading

- Dave Andrews, *Christi-Anarchy* (Lion, 2001).
- Tom Wright, *Surprised by Hope* (Society for Promoting Christian Knowledge, 2005).

Suggested Questions for Further Discussion/Thought

1. Is the primary focus of the Christian life here and now, or on the afterlife?
2. What makes heaven an important concept to people? What about hell?
3. Why is going to heaven the wrong question if you pray as Jesus commanded in Matthew 5:9–13?
4. Is grace inclusive or exclusive? Is its purpose to weed out the riffraff or to embrace the undeserving?
5. If there are any conditions at all, is it really grace?

Why would stories about a father murdering his daughter (Judg. 11) or handing his daughters over to a crowd to be raped and killed (Gen. 19) be included in the Bible?

....

Gary Peluso-Verdend

The victors who write history often conceal crimes, immorality, and misdeeds. For the most part, that is not so in the Bible! Biblical stories tend to report warts and all, even for beloved leaders such as King David (see 2 Sam. 11–12). With the possible exception of Jesus (and even there you have his initial treatment of the Syrophoenician woman; see Mk. 7:25–30), one cannot find flawless leaders in the Bible.

Rather, we have many stories of sometimes-honored persons making terrible decisions and acting in horrific, unethical, or cowardly ways. In Judges 11, Jephthah made a stupid vow to God that cost the life of his only daughter. Genesis 19 includes the story of Lot offering up his daughters to a mob rather than surrendering the guests who were under the protection of his house.

So why are such stories included in the Bible? New Testament scholar Doug Adams claims the Bible does not present us with models for morality, but mirrors for identity. We are to look for ourselves in biblical stories and see what and who is reflected back. Such reflections help us deal with the people around us and with ourselves, if we can look deeply enough into our souls. For example, check out Jesus' family tree as Matthew 1:1–16 reports it—enough flawed characters in there for a TV drama.

Bible stories may not always point in a "go thou and do likewise" direction, but are sometimes markers for what not to do.

....

Marcia Ford

One thing you can say about the Bible—it never whitewashes the evil that humans are capable of doing to one another. But because so much of the Bible teaches love and offers comfort, it's hard for some people to relate to those passages that depict gruesome and despicable actions.

However, the Bible is much more than a source of feel-good reassurance. It's also a record of the history of Israel and the early church, and that record is populated by very real people who sometimes exemplified the essence of evil.

Why are those stories included? The Jewish and Christian leaders who determined the canon of scripture were careful not to censor its words. They believed that each book they considered to be canonical was the true word of God and should not be tampered with. They insisted on leaving in the good, the bad, and the ugly.

In addition to the accounts of brutality against individuals and the atrocities perpetrated against entire clans, the Bible also records the thoughts of violence and cruelty that men harbored against others, particularly those in what are called the "imprecatory" psalms. Those psalms openly express the psalmist's desire to exact vengeance on his enemies as well as the enemies of God.

Along with the vicious accounts, these psalms provide us with a stark contrast to the teachings of Jesus about loving our enemies—and with the hope that even the most evil people can be transformed by God's power.

....

Kathy Escobar

A. I have absolutely no idea why God includes such bizarre, painful, extremely contradictory stories in the Bible. The Bible is a raw, unedited version of humanity and divinity mixed together. These horrific stories remind us of what we as people are capable of. They offer a constant reminder that real life is ugly, dark, self-absorbed, and dangerous, and that left on our own many of us will do things we had no idea we were actually capable of doing.

At the same time, we cannot dismiss that there are passages in the Old Testament that point toward God actually directing people to do what we'd call fairly horrific things, like wipe out entire villages of people. I don't have a simple way to make sense of those scriptures. They hurt. They confuse me if I focus in on them for too long and forget to turn my attention to the bigger story—God's incredible heart and his passionate pursuit of people.

Regardless of the weird, unexplainable ways that God's stories are recorded in the scriptures, the Holy Spirit is alive and well, working through flawed, messed up, confused people.

I cannot dismiss that those passages are there, nor can I dismiss that amid the rubble and pain and destruction of life this side of heaven, there is also so much beauty and redemption. I have come to believe that the weird, unexplainable paradoxes in the Bible are a reflection of the weird, unexplainable paradoxes in us as people.

We are both good and bad, light and darkness, sinner and saint. And so are some of these stories in the Bible.

....
Rebecca Bowman Woods

These are two of the most horrific stories in the Bible, especially for women. I was talking with my friend Amy, who is in the process of being ordained as a Reform Jewish rabbi, about the "Banned Questions" project, and I asked her opinion on this one.

Amy pointed out that many of these painful stories about women are in the context of family, and within families, people often hurt each other. Lot verbally offers his daughters to an angry mob of men outside his home. They ignore Lot's offer and try to break the door down to get to the two angels who are inside. No thanks to Lot, his daughters are spared.

Jephthah vows that if God helps him win a battle, he will sacrifice to God "whoever comes out of the doors of my house to meet me, when I return victorious." He probably expected to see an animal first, not his only child. He keeps his vow, but he allows his daughter to spend two months in the mountains, "bewailing her virginity" with her friends. Without any children, she believes that she will not be remembered.

Maybe that's the point. Stories like these need to be remembered. They stand alongside the stories of women who have been victims of violence down through the ages and even today, challenging us to make the world a better, safer place for women and girls.

Parts of the Bible paint a picture of the world as God intends the world to be. Other parts describe the world as it is. We don't move any closer to the former by removing the latter.

• • • • • •

Scriptural References

Genesis 19:6–8; Judges 11:29–40; Proverbs 10:12; 17:9; 25:21–22; Luke 6:27–35; John 13:34–35; Romans 12:9–10; Galatians 5:6; Philippians 1:9–11; 1 Peter 4:8; 1 John 3:14; 4:7–21

Suggested Additional Sources for Reading

- Douglas Adams, *The Prostitute in the Family Tree* (Westminster John Knox Press, 1997).
- George Fox, *The Journal of George Fox* (Friends United Press, 2006).
- Phyllis Tribble, *Texts of Terror: Literary-Feminist Readings of Biblical Narratives* (Fortress Press, 1984).

Suggested Questions for Further Discussion/Thought

1. Imagine if the Bible didn't include all of these hard and disturbing stories. Would it make you like it more or less? Why?

2. How can the violent episodes recorded in the Bible enhance your understanding of human nature? How can they help you come to terms with the darker side of your own nature?

3. Why do you think God would have wanted unsavory passages included in the Bible?

4. Do you believe that the stories in Judges 11 and Genesis 19 reflect God's will?

5. What is the relationship between forgiving and forgetting? Are they the same thing?

Why would God send Jesus as the sacrificial lamb of God, dying for the sins of the world, instead of just destroying sin or perhaps offering grace and forgiveness to the very ones created by God? Why does an all-powerful being need a mediator anyway?

....

Chris Haw

I have found it important for my mind to get the "sacrificial lamb" idea back into working shape by, for example, considering how Jesus also died *from the sins of the world*. A terrible steamroller of mob violence, groupthink, and sacred violence struck down Jesus—as it struck down many others. A multitude of our sins, not God, killed Jesus. What is hopeful, however, is how he did not squirm under the temptations to violate love (even toward his enemy) and reduce himself to the level of his torturers and accusers. This fortuitous and righteous display of love is not tangential to his mission—for *God is love*. This witness is salvific not only because it is a good example to live by—which it is—but also because it is *now part of the human story*. Humanity has a chance—for at least *one* of its members lived in truth.

As to a "mediator" this seems (at least) like a confusion of words: Forgiveness needs mediation like a sentence needs words. When I forgive you for stealing my couch, I need the mediation of an action or a word to make my forgiveness real—or else it is mere sentiment in my mind. But to go even further beyond a mediated forgiveness, and enter into truth and reconciliation, you are going to need to also return my couch! Is that not how the metaphor of the "Word of God made flesh" works? We need at least one human not only to receive God's mercy—which has been latent in the universe since before it began—but also to return God's couch, so to speak; Jesus, the tradition seems to say, is the human to have done so.

And for what it is worth, the "sending his son" verse should not be understood as God killing someone. (Did God's denunciation of human sacrifice not begin with the binding of Isaac?) No, *We* killed God's Son, and it was sinful and unjust; Jesus' freely accepting his (pseudolegal) mob scapegoating does not legitimize it but instead attempts to overcome it with love. Thus John 3:16–21 should be understood constructively as God sending us righteousness incarnate—the way of true love in visible expression—not a great person to torture and satiate a bloodlust.

····················

Lee C. Camp

A. There is a long and complex tradition of varying interpretations of the meaning of the death of Jesus. The early church primarily thought of the death of Jesus as a victory over the powers of sin and death. Sin was not understood merely as the willful act of breaking God's rules, but as a power that enslaved and corrupted God's good creation. Personified in Satan, that power was always pulling humans down to the grave, punishment, and wrath. In Jesus, God overcame the rebellious powers through suffering love.

In the medieval era, another trajectory became predominant in the West. Anselm of Canterbury argued that a God-man was necessitated because of the great gravity of sin: Sin dishonored God, and humankind had to make some reparation, some *satisfaction* for sin. Humankind was unable to make such a repayment, and thus Jesus became the substitute, restoring the honor due to God through his obedience unto death. By the sixteenth century, John Calvin focused on *punishment*: Because of the immensity of humankind's sin, God's wrath demanded punishment. Jesus became the substitute punishment.

Peter Abelard, a contemporary with Anselm, argued that it was neither reparation nor punishment that God demanded, but repentance. Thus the loving example of Jesus effects a change in the heart of humankind, bringing about such repentance.

There has been renewed attention to this doctrine in the last number of decades: Numerous interpreters are assessing the variety in the Christian tradition not as mutually exclusive and competing interpretations but as metaphors—each having its own particular strengths and weaknesses— that give us different glimpses of the profound historical fact of a crucified Messiah.

·······················

Jarrod McKenna

A. Ever read Leviticus 16? Odd text. Yet French anthropologist René Girard reminds us that, despite how primitive Leviticus 16 might seem to us, every culture creates "scapegoats."

Scapegoats are those we blame to keep us in the dark to what has shaped us, namely, the systems that demand victims. Nero put early Christians to the stake. Europe burnt powerful women as witches. Magisterial reformers drowned the Anabaptists. Colonizers deliberately infected indigenous peoples with smallpox. Nazis took millions of Jews to the gas chambers. Jim Crow America lynched black America. The Australian government imprisons "boat people" seeking refuge. A Christian school fires a teacher because of her sexual orientation despite her passion for Jesus. To maintain their place in the "cool group," kids universally seek out and identify "geeks." Guantanamo tortures innocents, fearing they are terrorists. All this is done to keep us "safe," to maintain "order," to protect "us," and restore "peace." In the face of this reality, *our* reality, "total depravity" seems optimistic.

The gospel is not that some deity takes out its rage on an innocent victim so he doesn't have to take it out on all of us eternally. This is a diabolical lie dressed up in Christian drag that reverses the gospel, making it the same old bad news, while concealing that Jesus is victorious over it. God doesn't need blood. God doesn't need a mediator. *We do!*

In Jesus, God knowingly becomes the scapegoat, as "the Lamb of God who takes away the sins of the world" (John 1:29). The lamb of God is *NOT* offered *to* God by humanity but *is God* offered to us to enable a new humanity. God is reconciling the world to Godself through Christ by knowingly becoming our victim, exposing this idolatrous system that promises order, safety, peace, and protection in exchange for victims. In the resurrection, we are all confronted with the grace of our Creator in the forgiving victim who sends the Holy Spirit to shape a new world where no more blood needs to be shed.

· · · · · · · · · · · · · · · · · · · ·

Christian Piatt

The two-dollar phrase for the concept raised in this question is "substitutionary atonement" or "blood atonement." The idea that the sacrifice of a living creature was required to appease God for one's sins has been around for a lot longer than Christianity has. Mentions of animal sacrifice can be found throughout the Old Testament, and Abraham's faith is even tested when he's asked to sacrifice his own son.

This value of sacrifice as part of one's faith was also common in the Roman culture, in which the types of sacrifices usually were specific to the characteristics of the gods being worshipped. So a god of the harvest would require an offering of produce, and so on. Some pre-Christian cultures, such as those from Carthage, even practiced human sacrifice, though the Romans generally condemned it.

In the fourth century C.E., Gregory of Nyssa proposed that Jesus' death was an act of liberation, freeing humanity from enslavement to Satan. Seven hundred years later, Anselm developed what was then known as the "satisfaction" concept, which is closest to what we think of now as atonement theology. Jesus, being both human and perfectly divine, was the only sacrifice that could appease the offense to God by human sin. This idea pointed to Romans and Galatians as support for this interpretation.

Around the same time, a theologian named Peter Abelard proposed that it actually was Jesus' response of pure—some might emphasize *nonviolent*—love in the face of violence, hatred, and death that was transformative in the human psyche, reorienting us toward a theology of sacrificial love over justice or atonement. Walter Wink has gone a step further and claimed that atonement theology is a corruption of the gospel, focusing on an act of violence rather than the values of peaceful humility and compassion lived and taught by Christ.

. . . .

Pablo A. Jiménez

A. Metaphors, metaphors; religious language is poetic. Given that God is "Other," we can hardly understand who God is. Therefore, we use metaphorical language in order to convey our ideas about God. This language is always contextual. This means that we usually compare God to things we know, particularly to creation. In theology, this is called the *analogia entis*, a Latin phrase, which means the "analogy of being."

Therefore, it should not surprise us that ancient religious language is based on metaphors. The question addresses three common metaphors. The first is an agricultural one, in which Jesus is compared to a lamb that is sacrificed for the benefit of the community. The second is a legal metaphor that compares the sinner with people condemned to death for their crimes. The third is a political image, which describes Jesus as the mediator between the people and God, the powerful King.

Every generation has the responsibility of rethinking the faith, searching for new and more effective metaphors to describe the relationship between God and humanity. However, before tossing out the old metaphors, we need to understand their meaning. In a way, theology is a dialogue across generations, time, and space. Before developing our own theological language, we must try to understand what other generations said about God, Jesus, and other common theological themes.

. . . .

Amy Reeder Worley

A. The idea that Jesus died as the "sacrificial lamb of God" is called "substitutionary atonement," which is a fancy way of saying that Jesus was crucified as a sacrifice to pay the "sin debt" of humanity. Although for many Christians atonement is essential to Christianity, it wasn't articulated fully until a thousand years *after* Jesus' death in a treatise by

Anselm of Canterbury. Regrettably, many people are unaware of a body of biblical scholarship skeptical of substitutionary atonement.

When trying to glean meaning from sacred texts, it helps to consider whatever knowledge we have about the writer, his political and social world, and to whom he wrote. For example, some cite Paul's letters as supporting substitutionary atonement. However, when we read Paul in context, we understand two important things. First, Paul wrote to early Christians during the first century C.E., long before Anselm's exposition on atonement. Second, Paul was a practicing Jew during a time in Jewish history when believers sacrificed animals at the Temple, seeking forgiveness for violations of the law.

Given his religious heritage, it is unsurprising that Paul borrowed from the Jewish tradition of sacrificial atonement. The use of atonement-related language does not necessarily mean, however, that Paul thought Jesus was literally a sacrificial lamb for humankind.

I would argue that substitutionary atonement is logically inconsistent with Paul's writing about a loving and compassionate God who freely bestows grace on the world. Reading Paul as a Jew writing under Roman imperial rule, we can see him trying to teach early Christians about *the interrelation* of Jesus' crucifixion *and* resurrection.

Rome executed Jesus in part because of his radically antiestablishment message, and because some believed he sought political power. I believe that Jesus was crucified *because of human sin, not in the place of humans who sin.* Because of the resurrection, Jesus (and his followers) ultimately defeats death and arises victorious.

Paul summarized this view of Jesus' death and resurrection when he urged early Christians to "die" to sin and "live again in" Christ.

• • • • • •

Scriptural References

Leviticus 16; Mark 10:35–45; Luke 11:49–51; John 10:33; Romans 3:24–25; 6:19–23; 12:2; 1 Corinthians 1:17—2:16; 2 Corinthians 5:18–21; Galatians 3: 1–14; Hebrews 10:10

Suggested Additional Sources for Reading

- James Alison, *Knowing Jesus* (Templegate, 1994).
- James Alison, *The Joy of Being Wrong* (Crossroad, 1998).
- René Girard, *I See Satan Fall Like Lightning* (Orbis, 1991).
- Karen Armstrong, *The Battle for God* (Ballantine, 2001).
- Gustaf Aulen, *Christus Victor* (Macmillan, 1931).

- Marcus Borg, *Jesus: Uncovering the Life, Teachings, and Relevance of a Religious Revolutionary* (HarperSanFrancisco, 2006).
- Marcus Borg and John Crossan, *The First Paul: Reclaiming the Radical Visionary Behind the Church's Conservative Icon* (HarperOne, 2009).
- Walter Wink, *Jesus and Nonviolence: A Third Way* (Fortress Press, 2003).
- Walter Wink, *The Powers That Be: Theology for a New Millennium* (Doubleday, 1998).
- Paul Tillich, *Systematic Theology*, vol. 2 (Univ. of Chicago Press, 1957).
- Joel B. Green and Mark D. Baker, *Recovering the Scandal of the Cross: Atonement in the New Testament and Contemporary Contexts* (InterVarsity, 2000).
- James Wm. McClendon Jr., "The Saving Cross: Atonement" in *Systematic Theology*, vol. 2, *Doctrine* (Abingdon Press, 1994).
- Brad Jersak and Michael Hardin, *Stricken by God?: Nonviolent Identification and the Victory of Christ* (Eerdmans, 2007).

Suggested Questions for Further Discussion/Thought

1. What stories have you heard preachers tell to explain the meaning of Jesus' crucifixion? Which one of the traditions of interpretation does that story illustrate?
2. Does this view of the crucifixion challenge your faith?
3. Does it lend more or less credibility to the Christian faith?
4. Does it make Jesus' death any less relevant to Christianity?
5. Were you raised with the idea that Jesus died for your sins? How has this influenced your understanding of the Christian faith?
6. Do you believe that God would condone sacrificing a man in payment for the sins of the world? Why or why not?
7. Have you encountered arguments against, or alternatives to, atonement theology? What do you think of them?

Many Christians embrace the phrase, "I believe Jesus is the Christ, the son of the living God, and I accept him as my personal Lord and Savior," but I can't find this anywhere in the Bible. Where did it come from?

....

Amy Reeder Worley

I sometimes dream those words—a refrain carved in my memory. I'm haunted by the voice of my congregation repeating the gospel hymn "Just as I Am" until someone went to the altar to pray. My pastor's hands and voice were high as he demanded, "Have YOU accepted Jesus Christ as YOUR personal Lord and Savior? Have YOU asked the Lord's forgiveness and become a Christian?"

As a girl, I was taught that the Bible said, without any other possible interpretation, there is one God, one faith, one baptism, and one way to God the Father via his son Jesus Christ, who died on the cross *because of my sins*. Those who did not have a "personal relationship" with Jesus were not saved. Not saved meant being doomed to hell.

I ultimately had to leave the church for years to exorcise this theology. And I still haven't completely lost the involuntary guilt it left in me. Those words, putting Jesus' death and the state of my soul in my small hands, are etched in my cells, leaving me somehow a bit wounded.

The distressing part of this message is that it puts all of Christianity on the Christian. It is graceless. The emphasis on a "personal" relationship with Jesus implies that salvation is somehow entirely self-initiated.

I don't believe that was Jesus' message. Jesus said that no one gets to the Father but through him. But he also said to follow him because he was *of* God and *knew* God. Jesus spoke of God's unconditional love, which is available to all who are open to receive it. God's love is not ours personally; it's communal. Jesus spoke about the kingdom of God and there cannot be a kingdom of one.

I have an Anne Lamott quote on my computer that sums it up for me. She says, "I do not at all understand the mystery of grace—only that it meets us where we are but does not leave us where it found us." God comes to us, not just "I," but "us"—all of us. That is the very nature of grace. Our relationship with God is by its very nature not personal but collective.

Chris Haw

The phrase comes from a conglomeration of excerpts from the book of Romans, Peter's confession in Mark, and a few other places. But nowhere does the modifier "personal Lord" makes it into the New Testament as this is a misnomer: "Lords" are by their nature public and political beings. More important, as many scholars are now admitting, to call Jesus your "Lord and Savior" in the first century is to say, "Caesar is not."

The phrase invites (nearly sarcastic) political provocation and paradox through the exaltation of the humiliated and crucified "Lord." The phrase means, I exalt the humbled, or I give power to the powerless one, or I favor the unfavored, or I love the unloved, and so on.

Jarrod McKenna

The "Sinners' Prayer" is not in the Bible. Variations of it arose in the Great Awakenings, when evangelists were helping people make faith personal. God is gracious and will work with anything, but there is a very real danger today in our hyperindividualistic cultures that the Sinners' Prayer can become a magic incantation to avoid hell rather than something that helps us live as a prayer in response to the grace God has shown us.

The early Christians did not pray the Sinners' Prayer as isolated individuals to become Christians. They prayed the Lord's Prayer as communities in response to the grace of God. They responded to the gospel by becoming part of such a people by entering into the waters of baptism. More than just a personal prayer, baptism was a political changing of allegiances, facilitating the death of the nationalism, patriotism, racism, violence, lust, and greed that named us. Through baptism, the early Christians were raised in the name of the Triune God (Matthew 28:19, Galatians 3:26–29) to walk as Jesus walked (1 John 2:6) and were immersed in the narrative of God's liberating work throughout history, of which Christ is the culmination. They were immersed in the reality of the repentance, forgiveness of sins, and the gift of the Holy Spirit of God's future (Acts 2:38), birthed anew into God's New World breaking in (John 3:3–5, 1 Peter 1:3, Titus 3:5).
They died to their old selves, formed in the patterns of the kingdoms of this world, and were raised with Christ into the nonviolent redemptive patterns of discipleship (Romans 6:3–11, Colossians 2:12).

In doing so they didn't merely invite Jesus into their heart as their personal Lord and Savior. More than that, they responded to Jesus' invitation to enter into God's heart to heal all of creation. It was not merely an outward sign of an inner reality; it was a personal appropriation of the outward coming of the kingdom of God. They pledged allegiance to Christ as cosmic Lord and Savior of all creation (1 Peter 3:21). As evangelists, we are commissioned to invite the world to pray the Lord's Prayer with us as we witness to the kingdom coming on earth (Matthew 6:9–13).

....

R. M. Keelan Downton

While I've never heard it in that particular form, the first part comes from an exchange between Peter and Jesus recorded in the gospel of Matthew. Jesus first asks what other people are saying about him and then asks, *but who do you say I am?* The significance of Jesus as personal savior is more the product of nineteenth- and twentieth-century reflection of certain parts of the church. The adjective "personal" was used to distinguish those seeking to cultivate spiritual life through intentional practices (the *method* of Methodism, though they were not the only ones to do so) from the impersonal deist god of the enlightenment that motivated so many of the "founding fathers" of the United States.

It later came to interact with the hyperindividualism of liberal democratic capitalism to make encounters with God another commoditized expression of identity, like jeans or a cell phone case (also the source of "worship" songs that leave the uninitiated unsure whether you are referring to Jesus or a girlfriend).

There is something important in the idea that Jesus came for *me*, but in a culture that's already so focused on "me," we probably need a little more focus on Jesus as the Messiah or Christ who came to challenge the apparent order of the world and invite us to join in the process of revealing the true order of the world by proclaiming and embodying it.

• • • • • •

Scriptural References

Matthew 6:9–13; 28:19; John 3:3–5; Acts 2:38; Romans 6:3–11; Galatians 3:26–29; Colossians 2:12; Titus 3:5; 1 Peter 1:3; 3:21; 1 John 2:6

Suggested Additional Sources for Reading

- Henry Nouwen, *The Return of the Prodigal Son* (Continuum, 1995).
- Anne Lamott, *Grace Eventually, Thoughts on Faith* (Riverhead, 2007).
- George Lindbeck, *The Nature of Doctrine: Religion and Theology in a Postliberal Age* (Westminster, 1984).
- Susan Campbell, *Dating Jesus: A Story of Fundamentalism, Feminism, and the American Girl* (Beacon, 2009).
- Fredrick Buechner, *The Alphabet of Grace* (Harper & Row, 1970).

- Margaret Atwood, *The Handmaid's Tale* (McLelland & Stewart, 1985).
- Gregory A. Boyd, *The Myth of a Christian Religion* (Zondervan, 2009).
- Lee Camp, *Mere Discipleship* (Brazos Press, 2003).
- John H. Yoder, *Body Politics* (Discipleship Resources, 1992).
- N. T. Wright, *Jesus and the Victory of God* (Augsburg Fortress Press, 1997).

Suggested Questions for Further Discussion/Thought

1. Do you believe faith is personal or communal?
2. Amy's piece speaks about being wounded by a theological message. Have you ever experienced that? Is healing possible?
3. What do you understand about grace? Can we ever "deserve" it?
4. What does it say about God if salvation is only available to those who accept church dogma?
5. What if instead of inviting people to pray the Sinners' Prayer, we invited them to pray the Lord's Prayer and to explore what emersion into God's New World might mean for them? How would this change the way we share the gospel?

In John 14:6, Jesus says, "I am the way, and the truth, and the life. No one comes to the Father except through me." Do people have to choose to follow Jesus to go to heaven? And what does it mean to choose his way?

....
Phil Snider

A lot of people think this verse means that only those who accept Jesus into their heart as their personal Lord and Savior will go to heaven. But if you read the gospels closely, you'll see that Jesus never mentions this as a requirement for salvation. I tend to think that faith in Jesus should make us more inclusive of others rather than less. While people are quite good at building walls of exclusion, it's the upside-down kingdom of God announced by Jesus that knocks them down time and again, precisely because Jesus' way—in stark contrast to our own—is "the truth, and the life." Accordingly, heaven can be viewed as that place and time (no matter which side of the grave you happen to be on) in which God's love reigns supreme.

Furthermore, I don't think that choosing Christ is a one-time affair, but rather a decision I make (or don't make) every moment of my life. As Peter Rollins suggests, I choose Christ's way "when I stand up for those who are forced to live on their knees, when I speak for those who have had their tongues torn out, when I cry for those who have no more tears left to shed,"[1] *yet I deny Christ every time I don't*. So you might say I'm aspiring to be a Christian, and in the best moments of my life, as few and as far between as they are, I hope to become one.

....
Chris Haw

John's mysterious gospel also mentions that no one can "choose Jesus" except by being drawn by the Father. Perhaps one might think that John was anachronistically agreeing with Calvinism's predestination or Augustinianism.

I think it is best to interpret John's point in light of the larger scope of his theology. The best way to interpret this verse is to understand what Jesus is to John: Jesus has God's full life in him. And that life is *love*—for "God is love."

Simply, if you do not have the life of God in you, you cannot go on living after your biological life gives way. This isn't a matter of exclusion; it is a way of identifying the principle by which life persists: God's being, which is love. Admittedly this position, intermingled as it is with the resurrection of the dead, appears to us as extremely optimistic—that love animates life.

In popular imagery, we have retained this thought by symbolizing the heart with love—not an obvious connection when you think about it. Perhaps even more interestingly, we have some biological findings that should give us pause when we declare our modern veto on all miracles and our ban on the resurrection: "At the organismal level, there are no physiological or thermodynamic reasons why death must occur. In fact, there are several unicellular species that are immortal and one advanced multicellular organism that has not demonstrated any signs of senescence (Bristlecone Pine)."[2]

So from a certain perspective, "choosing Jesus" means choosing life, which means choosing love. But love is a profoundly confused term and begs not only a definition but also a specific example. Jesus is apparently our most excellent example of love. Therefore, if you reject him, you are rejecting love. I appreciate how the church has maintained a canon of saints to clarify other echoes of Jesus, so we keep our minds tuned to what "accepting Jesus" looks like.

. . . .

Peter J. Walker

Historically, Christianity has taught a fairly exclusive doctrine of salvation: Those who don't accept Christ are condemned to hell. That teaching is easier to accept when you are (a) an oppressed believer, living under violent persecution or (b) part of a theocratic society where *everyone* is Christian. In either scenario, it's unlikely that typical Christians faced the dilemma of a neighbor or loved one who did not believe. That's probably a core reason our soteriology (study of religious doctrines of salvation) developed and cemented as it did. In the twenty-first century, however, we confront this problem daily with friends, family, coworkers, and classmates.

There are plenty of scriptures available for constructing arguments in favor of exclusivism, inclusivism, and universalism. No one "wins" that fight. We all choose to believe what seems true to us. Many of the most conservative Christians I have known still make special allowances for people they care about—people who "couldn't possibly go to hell!"

Objective truth is one thing; subjective relationships are another. My friend Jim Henderson (http://www.offthemap.com) says, "When people like each other, the rules change." Many of these changed rules remain secret because people are scared of risking judgment or reproach from their churches. I have decided to accept the backlash and make my rule breaking public because I think it's helpful to talk about these things openly.

I know that my salvation is in Christ, but I don't demand that of others. If Jesus came only to offer exclusive salvation through himself, then he actually made things worse for folks, not better. I believe Jesus flung the door to God wide open! George Fox, the founder of Quakerism, referred to an "inner light" that every human being carries: God's immediate presence. I affirm that spiritual connection in us all, and believe it is inherently salvific.

Sherri Emmons

This is one of the hardest passages in the New Testament for me, because it seems to run counter to so many of Jesus' other teachings about compassion and forgiveness. I have a hard time imagining a God who would turn away people because they didn't follow a particular way or didn't even know about that way.

If we take seriously the image of God as a father, then we have to believe God loves his children. As a mother, I cannot imagine any sin so horrific that I would condemn my children to everlasting damnation. Surely God is not a worse parent than I am.

A friend shared a metaphor about heaven that makes a lot of sense to me. We are all climbing a mountain toward the kingdom of God, and there are many different paths we can follow. Not all of them reach the top. Some lead to dead ends. Some lead to disaster. But I believe there is more than one path to the top. And Jesus himself gave us a road map when he said, "Thus you will know them by their fruits" (Matthew 7:20).

Amy Reeder Worley

John is the newest and most unique of the gospels. Although none of the gospels were written as purely historical accounts of the life and times of Jesus, John is the most mythical (truth revealed through the totality of a narrative rather than a logical theorem) and mystical (the pursuit of union with the Divine).

Because John differs from the synoptics (Matthew, Mark, and Luke) in its Christology and language, there is substantial scholarly disagreement about its ultimate message. However, most scholars agree that the author of John's view of Jesus is revelatory—Jesus came to reveal the path to God. In John, Jesus claims to be "the bread of life" (6:35), "the light of the world" (8:12), "the Advocate" (or "paraclete") (14:16), and "the life" (14:6). This metaphorical language evokes images of Jesus feeding the spiritually hungry, lighting the path for those who cannot see it, and drawing our attention to the sacred around us.

We should note that Jesus does not say, "no one gets to *heaven* but through me." Rather, he refers to getting to the Father. This is in keeping with John's somewhat mystical theology concerning the human experience of God. Second, although the second sentence of John 14:6 asserts the exclusivity of Jesus as the path to God, the first sentence explains *why* Jesus is the "way" to God. Jesus is the" truth," meaning his message was true. Jesus is the "life," meaning his life was a map to experience God. In other words according to John's gospel, Jesus embodied the way to God.

So is Jesus the *only* way to God? I don't think so. John was written during a time when the early Christian church sought legitimacy. It was distinguishing itself from Judaism and the Roman cults. I like to view the exclusive language in John 14:6 as an emphatic affirmation of the truth in Jesus' message, not a condemnation of other paths to God.

• • • • • •

Scriptural References

John 6:35; 8:12; 14:6; 14:16; Romans 5:18; Philippians 2:10–11; 1 Timothy 4:10

Suggested Additional Sources for Reading

- Douglas John Hall, *Why Christian? For Those on the Edge of Faith* (Fortress Press, 1998).

- Danielle Shroyer, *The Boundary-Breaking God: An Unfolding Story of Hope and Promise* (Jossey-Bass, 2009).

- Peter Rollins, *The Orthodox Heretic* (Paraclete Press, 2009).

- Eric Stetson, *Christian Universalism: God's Good News for All People* (Sparkling Bay, 2008).

- H. Larry Ingle, *First among Friends: George Fox and the Creation of Quakerism* (Oxford Univ. Press, 1994).

- Marcus J. Borg, *The Heart of Christianity: Rediscovering a Life of Faith* (HarperSanFrancisco, 2003).

- The Christian Universalist Association: http://www.christianuniversalist .org.

- Philip Gulley and James Mulholland, *If Grace Is True: Why God Will Save Every Person* (HarperSanFrancisco, 2003).

Suggested Questions for Further Discussion/Thought

1. If you affirm faith in Jesus Christ as God's representative, does that make you more or less inclusive of others?

2. Do you believe that God's love transcends doctrines, creeds, and religions? If so, how does that affect the way you view non-Christian religions? Does such a perspective diminish God's love or expand God's love?

3. Is it possible to be on Christ's way even if you don't believe in God? Is it possible to be transformed by God if you don't believe in God?

4. When we talk about heaven what do you think most people mean?

5. What about Jesus made him "the way, and the truth, and the life"?

6. How does John's Jesus differ from the Jesus of the synoptics?

7. Does a religion need to be *exclusively* true to be true?

What happened during the "missing years" of Jesus' life, unaccounted for in the Bible?

....

Becky Garrison

Beats me. While biblical archeologists and historians have pieced together evidence illuminating the life and times of first century Judeans, we have no clue about what Jesus actually did until he begins his ministry.

We can assume that as a good Jewish boy, he probably assisted his father in the carpentry biz though there's no concrete evidence that Jesus became a carpenter. Also, Jesus deviated from the vast majority of his neighbors by receiving some type of an education as evidenced by his vast knowledge of the Hebrew Scriptures.

As Scott Korb points out, "Presumably if you're sitting with scholars discussing theology, you probably know how to read and write."[3] But given that Jesus grew up in an oral culture that valued the spoken over the written word, he might have learned aurally instead.

....

L. Shannon Moore

The only things we know from the Bible about Jesus as a child are found in the book of Luke. As a baby he was named, circumcised, and presented in the temple. Then, at the age of twelve, he accompanied his parents to Jerusalem for the Passover festival and ditched them to chat with the teachers in the Temple.

Now there are some other written gospels that weren't chosen by the early church leaders to make the final cut of the Bible. One of my favorites is called the infancy gospel of Thomas. Written about 125 C.E., it was "devoted to filling the gap left by some of the other gospels."[4] These stories are crazy! For example,

- Boy Jesus gets in trouble for making clay birds on the Sabbath so he claps his hands, and they turn into real birds and fly away.

- Another kid bumps into Jesus, making him angry. So Jesus yells at him and the kid falls down dead.

- Jesus' father, a carpenter, is making a bed for a rich man and cuts a piece of wood too short. Jesus simply stretches the shorter piece out to match the longer piece.

While these stories make for fun reading, I don't buy them for a second. I think Jesus grew up like all the other boys in his town—going to the synagogue, doing his chores, and so on—and did not possess (or was unaware) of any divine power until after his baptism.

....

Mark Van Steenwyk

Jesus' life is a big question mark. The gospels mostly tell us about the three years leading up to Jesus' crucifixion. We also know a fair bit about his birth and infancy. We even get an interesting story about Jesus wowing scholars at the temple when he was twelve. But what did he do between the age of twelve and the age of thirty? This is one of those really juicy mysteries that provoke all sorts of speculation.

Most scholars assume that Jesus grew up in Nazareth and learned carpentry. Some say Jesus traveled to India, Nepal, Tibet, or China and soaked up the mojo of Eastern Buddhist mystics. Others say he traveled back to Egypt and learned the wisdom of Egyptian spiritual teachers. But all we really know from the gospels comes from Luke 2:52 where we read, "And Jesus increased in wisdom and in years, and in divine and human favor."

The idea that Jesus had to travel to the East to learn how to be a sage is a bit snobby. Why is it so hard for folks to believe that some peasant kid from occupied Israel could grow up to be the most revered spiritual leader in history without getting some sort of outside help?

The guy was born in a barn! It is only fitting to assume that Jesus grew up humbly and became a blue-collar worker. Throughout his whole life and ministry, the amazing thing about Jesus was that—through it all—he was, from a human perspective, something of a loser. And perhaps even more amazing, he tells us that the kingdom of God belongs to other losers. In other words, we don't need to learn from sages or mystics to be a part of the "big things" that God wants to do in the world today.

• • • • • •

Scriptural References

Luke 2:39–52; 3:23

Suggested Additional Sources for Reading

- Elaine Pagels, *Beyond Belief: The Secret Gospel of Thomas* (Vintage, 2004).
- Christopher Moore, *Lamb: The Gospel According to Biff, Christ's Childhood Pal* (Harper, 2003).

- Scott Korb, *Life in Year One: What the World Was Like in First-Century Palestine* (Riverhead, 2010).
- David R. Cartlidge and David L. Dungan, eds., "The Infancy Gospel of Thomas," in *Documents for the Study of the Gospels* (Augsburg Fortress Press, 1994).

Suggested Questions for Further Discussion/Thought

1. Why do you think some people suggest that Jesus' teachings were borrowed from Buddha?

2. Where do you think Jesus went for the eighteen "missing years"?

3. Do you think Jesus possessed, or was aware of, his divine power when he was a child? If so, would it have been in his nature to use them in the ways presented in the infancy gospel of Thomas?

Why should I believe that Jesus was resurrected? What does it mean to the Christian faith if he wasn't resurrected?

···················
Peter J. Walker

A. The church has consistently affirmed the literal resurrection throughout history, defending it as central dogma. I affirm it too, but I have a hunch that you can personally know Jesus, either way. Theologian Rudolf Bultmann argued that the literal resurrection was less important than the story behind the myth. He believed that the power of the resurrection for modern believers is in its theological meaning—in what it said about the nature of God and the human condition. Bultmann stressed the importance of *choosing* faith rather than believing faith is somehow inevitable once "proven" legitimate.

So you don't *have* to believe that Jesus of Nazareth was resurrected. But if you can't at least believe that Jesus *might* have been resurrected, maybe we should talk about why. To me, a worldview bound by some notion of rigid Newtonian physics seems less creative, less dynamic, and less interesting than faith open to the supernatural. It's another kind of fundamentalism. I want to be able to dream dreams and hear whispers in the dark, even if I never see someone walk on water or heal the blind.

Deism, keeping God passive and separate from the workings of creation, certainly makes the problem of suffering more palatable. But there's something about Jesus more compelling than a moral philosophy or historic "high point" of humanity. There's more to Jesus than wisdom. I choose belief in a God who "can"—a God willing to be weak, to suffer and die. It's very existential. If God did or did not, that is less important to me. A God who at least *can* is a God who can reach me.

····························
Amy Reeder Worley

A. Most of us have heard the atheist critique of the resurrection of Jesus. "Zombie Jesus" is one pop culture reference to the secular humanist/ atheist's view of what they claim is the utter ridiculousness of the Christian belief that Jesus of Nazareth was crucified, died, and came back to life on the third day. Likewise, my disbelief in a literal resurrection of Jesus was one of many reasons I left the faith for years. I cannot adhere to a "magic" religion that requires belief in scientifically impossible events. So Zombie Jesus wasn't for me.

When I came back to the study of Christianity as an adult, after a foray into Buddhism and Yoga, I came to a new understanding of the resurrection. Well, actually I came back to an old understanding of the Christian resurrection, one that predates the post-Enlightenment religious literalism. Like the many religious resurrection stories before Christianity (e.g., Isis and Osiris), Jesus' resurrection is a metaphor for the very real process of dying to one's old life and living again in Jesus.

Sometimes referred to as "participatory atonement," many nonevangelical Christians take the Pauline approach that we metaphorically die to our old, unenlightened ways and then rise again filled with the spirit of Christ. In Galatians 2:19–20 Paul writes, "I have been crucified with Christ; and it is no longer I who live, but it is Christ who lives in me."

In this way, the resurrection of Christ is central to the Christian faith. Practicing Christians try to model Jesus by dying to our selfish, distracted ways and remaking ourselves in Christ's image. So although the resurrection is of utmost importance to Christians, we need not take it literally in order to believe.

·······················

Jarrod McKenna

Last time I was arrested for resisting the ongoing wars in Iraq and Afghanistan the police officer said to me, and I quote, "You need to realize that war is money. And money makes the world go round. The sooner you realize that, the sooner you can fit in like the rest of us."

If Jesus wasn't resurrected, the police officer is right. The powers that crucified our Lord are right. We are still stuck in sin and in a closed sinful system that is fueled by, and profits from, the blood of our oppressed sisters and brothers. Our Lord's nonviolent way of the cross is not vindicated victorious over evil. There is no new world of God's kingdom breaking in, of which our Lord Jesus is the first fruits. Our faith is futile and we are to be pitied.

The hope of oppressed Jews of Jesus' day was *not* to be liberated from God's good creation; rather, they hoped for a material liberation from all injustice, violence, and oppression (Isaiah 2:2–4, 9:1–7, 11:6–9, 35:5–6, 60:17–19, and Micah 4:1–3, among others). They longed for that day when "God's Great Cosmic Clean-Up"[5] would kick-start with the righteous being raised to inherit the world-put-right. With a rationale echoing the words of the police officer, the Sadducees and Herodians sold out the revolutionary hope of resurrection because bodily resurrection will always threaten those who practice "spiritualities" that collaborate and profit from the powers' oppression.

The scandal of the bodily resurrection of Jesus (which N. T. Wright has persuasively argued as the most conceivable explanation for the birth and shape of the early church) is that the Jewish revolutionary hope has started! Yet scandalously, it's started through a crucified, nonviolent messiah in the middle of history. Now all creation waits in eager expectation for us to walk in the resurrection by taking up our cross, in the power of the Spirit, and witness to the end of all injustice, violence, oppression, and evil, which has now started because Jesus is risen from the grave.

········· ·············

L. Shannon Moore

We can look at the resurrection metaphorically. When we have Christ in our lives, the "old" self is resurrected into the "new" self. The worm becomes a butterfly; the egg becomes a bird; and the lost becomes the found. I get it.

But what about the physical resurrection of Jesus? My childhood Sunday school teacher would faint if she were to hear me say this, but I don't think it matters if Jesus rose from the dead or not. I do believe that Jesus, in human form, was the Son of God. And if he did rise from the grave, defeating death and sin and all things evil, I have no trouble believing that either. But if archaeologists were to discover his body in a tomb outside of Jerusalem tomorrow, it would not affect my faith. At all. Even though Christianity was born on that very idea (and acknowledging that untold millions have died defending that belief), I don't strive to pattern my life on the resurrection. I work toward following what Jesus taught, what he *said* and how he *lived* rather than on what happened after he died.

To be clear—until archaeologists actually do produce concrete, undeniable proof to the contrary, I choose to believe in the resurrection as it is told to us in the scriptures. But do I think that one has to believe in the resurrection to be a Christ follower? No.

········· ·············

Mark Van Steenwyk

The Apostle Paul wrote, "If Christ has not been raised, your faith is futile and you are still in your sins" (1 Corinthians 15:17). He also said that if Jesus wasn't raised, we won't be either. This would, he suggests, make our faith useless.

For the most part, I agree with Paul. The resurrection of Jesus not only gives us hope that we too will ultimately cheat death, but it also gives us hope that everything will be renewed—all death, degradation, sin, brokenness, sickness, and injustice will be transformed into something amazing.

Without that, would our faith be, as Paul suggests, useless? I'm not so sure. I'd still follow Jesus even if I were an atheist. Jesus has a lot to say about how to live in the here and now. Without the resurrection, we'd be left with a deeply challenging way to live our lives; a way that calls us to love our enemies, pursue justice, and seek peace. But we'd labor not knowing if we will be vindicated in our struggle. We'd go through life feeling the weight of our sins and the injustices of the world. That would be hard, but we could do far worse.

It would be worse for us to gain hope in the resurrection of Jesus and use it as an excuse for inaction. Because Jesus has defeated death, he is the true Lord of the whole world. Therefore we, his followers, have a job to do; we must act as his heralds, announcing his lordship to the entire world. Jesus is raised, therefore God's new world has begun, and therefore we are invited to be not only beneficiaries of that new world but participants in making it happen.

In his book *Worship and Politics*, Rafael Avila writes, "The resurrection is the ultimate basis for rebellion."[6] Ultimately, the resurrection gives us hope that, if we challenge the brokenness in the world, we will win.

● ● ● ● ● ●

Scriptural References

Isaiah 2:2–4; 9:1–7; 11:6–9; 35:5–6; 60:17–19; Micah 4:1–3; Matthew 28:1–10; Mark 16:1–11; Luke 24:1–12; John 20:1–8; Romans 6:3–4; 8; 12:2; 1 Corinthians 15; Galatians 2:19–20

Suggested Additional Sources for Reading

- Karen Armstrong, *The Case for God* (Knopf, 2009).
- John Shelby Spong, *Rescuing the Bible from Fundamentalism: A Bishop Rethinks the Meaning of Scripture* (HarperSanFrancisco, 1991).
- Marcus Borg and John Dominic Crossan, *The First Paul: Reclaiming the Radical Visionary Behind the Church's Conservative Icon* (HarperOne, 2009).
- N. T. Wright, *Jesus and the Victory of God* (Augsburg Fortress Press, 1997).
- Rudolph Bultmann, *Jesus Christ and Mythology* (Scribner, 1958).
- Marcus J. Borg, *The Heart of Christianity: Rediscovering a Life of Faith* (HarperSanFrancisco, 2003).
- Marcus J. Borg, *Meeting Jesus Again for the First Time: The Historical Jesus and the Heart of Contemporary Faith* (HarperSanFrancisco, 1994).
- Vintage Faith Church: http://www.vintagechurch.org.
- N. T. Wright, *The Resurrection of the Son of God* (SPCK, 2003).
- Lee C. Camp, *Mere Discipleship* (Brazos Press, 2003).

- Marcus Borg and N. T. Wright, *The Meaning of Jesus* (HarperOne, 2007).
- Robert B. Stewart, ed., *The Resurrection of Jesus: John Dominic Crossan and N. T. Wright in Dialogue* (Fortress Press, 2005).
- N. T. Wright, *Surprised by Hope* (HarperOne, 2008).
- Simon Barrow, *Threatened with Resurrection* (Darton, Longman, & Todd, 2008).

Suggested Questions for Further Discussion/Thought

1. Have you ever considered that being a Christian does not require belief in the literal resurrection of Jesus? Do you think that Christians must believe in the literal resurrection?

2. How does taking a metaphorical view of the resurrection affect your faith?

3. What were you originally taught about the resurrection?

4. How can we "know" Jesus—*God*, for that matter—without letting the beliefs, opinions or experiences of others overinfluence us?

5. Do we have to be sure of what we believe? What does it look like *not* to decide?

6. Is there a difference between being a "Christian" and being a "Christ follower?"

7. How revolutionary is your understanding of the resurrection?

Does it really matter if Jesus was born to a virgin or not? What if Mary wasn't a virgin or if Joseph (or someone else) was the father?

Amy Reeder Worley

Although many Christians disagree with me, I don't think belief in the literal virgin birth of Jesus is necessary to Christianity. Jesus was both fully human and fully divine whether or not he was born of a virgin. Jesus taught that we may all enter the kingdom of God, even though we're conceived by the usual means. Moreover, in describing his own relationship to God, Jesus did not rely on the virgin birth as proof of his divinity.

It is impossible to ever really know whether Mary was a virgin when she became pregnant with Jesus. However, we do know generally that conception requires that a sperm connect with an ovum to create an embryo. Could God create a virgin birth? Probably. Did God impregnate Mary by the Holy Spirit? Let's just say this—it wasn't necessary for God to do so for Jesus' message to be true.

As a woman and a feminist, my view of the virgin birth is complicated. Throughout the history of the church, the virgin birth has resulted in a view among some that women who are not sexually active should be adulated while sexually active women should be subjugated. This is often referred to in feminist scholarship as the "Madonna or the Whore" dichotomy. This dichotomy has caused sexually active women to feel unworthy of God's love and unable to fully experience it. The virgin birth also emphasizes the Divine's masculine attributes—the ability to cause pregnancy while ignoring the femininity of the Divine. These views have wounded the church universal, in particular its female members.

Jesus, however, included women in his ministry without reference to their sexual status. He bestowed mercy upon an adulterous woman. It was some combination of women to whom Jesus' resurrection was revealed. Accordingly, while we are certainly free to believe in a literal virgin birth, to do so is unnecessary.

Sherri Emmons

It doesn't matter to me if Jesus was born to a virgin. There are so many ancient tales in the Middle East of gods fathering children with virgins—the Greeks, Romans, and Egyptians all had such tales. So perhaps Jesus' original followers felt the need to "up" their prophet with that credential as well.

What does matter is what Jesus taught—love your enemies, love God with all your heart and soul, take care of those in need, and use your talents to serve God. The Christ I follow is one who calls me to act justly, speak truthfully, work tirelessly, and love endlessly. He lived those truths, even when it was hard and dangerous, and ultimately he died for them. That's what is important.

Peter J. Walker

It's easy to take for granted the early church's universal acknowledgement of Jesus' virgin conception based on its centrality in church tradition. But supported by scripture alone, it's surprising that Matthew and Luke were so unquestionably convinced, given that there is no other reference in the entire New Testament. The gospel accounts of Mark and John seem uninterested, and Paul didn't find it critical to his own apologetics.

"He [Jesus] was the son (as was thought) of Joseph" (Luke 3:23). *So it was thought* was good enough for Luke, but what about modern readers? Why are the genealogies so vastly different while both build through Joseph as Jesus' father? Was Joseph able to "adopt" Jesus into the Davidic line? Was Mary's virginity *constructed* to emphasize Jesus' divinity?

It surprises my friends when I ask these questions but still deliberately affirm the virgin conception. I am simultaneously aware of its unresolved difficulties and mindful of the power in its imagery and liturgical history. Many church doctrines have been diligently protected for two thousand years, and while I personally find little to call "nonnegotiable," I readily admit my own limitations.

Far more gifted, brilliant theologians have done battle before me, and in most cases, it doesn't hurt me to hold onto orthodox theology (lightly, with unclenched hands). I try to avoid rejecting traditional dogma outright unless it is used to exclude, abuse, or oppress others. In this vein, Mary's virginity has certainly had a complicated historical impact on women: simultaneously affirming their importance while narrowly restricting female sexual identity.

• • • • • •

Scriptural References

Matthew 1; Luke 1:26–38; 3

Suggested Additional Sources for Reading

- Elizabeth A. Johnson, *She Who Is* (Crossroad, 1992).
- Sue Monk-Kidd, *The Dance of the Dissident Daughter* (HarperSanFrancisco, 1996).
- Raymond Brown, *The Birth of the Messiah: A Commentary of the Infancy Narratives in the Gospels of Matthew and Luke* (Yale Univ. Press, 1999).
- Yigal Levin, "Jesus, 'Son of God' and 'Son of David': The 'Adoption' of Jesus into the Davidic Line," *Journal for the Study of the New Testament* 28, no. 4 (June 2006).
- Marcus J. Borg and John Dominic Crossan, *The First Christmas: What the Gospels Really Teach about Jesus's Birth* (HarperOne, 2009).
- Marguerite Rigoglioso, *The Cult of Divine Birth in Ancient Greece* (Palgrave Macmillan, 2009).
- J. Gresham Machen, *The Virgin Birth of Christ* (Harper and Bros., 1930).
- Roger Underwood, "The Virgin Birth: Why I Believe," *DisciplesWorld*, December 2003, 3–4.
- Jimmy R. Watson, "The Virgin Birth: Does It Matter?," *DisciplesWorld*, December 2003, 3, 5.

Suggested Questions for Further Discussion/Thought

1. Do you think the virgin birth story has affected the way the church views women?
2. If the virgin birth story is not literally true, how does that change your view of Jesus?
3. If you believe in the virgin birth, what impact does it have on your faith?
4. There are all sorts of questions in scripture that leave us hanging. How might answering those questions impact your spiritual journey? Which questions of faith are nonnegotiable for you?
5. What if Jesus was actually Joseph's biological son? Could Jesus still be God?

*Did Jesus really live a life without any sin?
What do we base this on? And does it
matter? Why?*

....

Pablo A. Jiménez

For people who understand sin as transgression, the idea of Jesus' "sinlessness" is ludicrous. Could anyone, including Jesus, live without sticking his or her hand in the forbidden cookie jar? Of course not! And once this basic tenet of the Christian faith falls to the ground, all other theological constructions must also tumble down.

Understanding sin as transgression leaves us with only two options. The first one is a Christology of moral example, where Jesus of Nazareth is viewed as an exemplary person, similar to Gandhi or Mother Theresa. The second option is a Christology that denies Jesus' humanity, affirming that his divine nature empowered him to live without transgressing.

However, the New Testament has another view of sin. It affirms that sin is a force or a state, more than a violation of the law. Being "in sin" implies being under the influence of the forces of death. Viewed from this standpoint, Jesus was indeed without sin because he was totally committed with God and with God's project for the world, God's kingdom or realm. His commitment was so strong that the forces of death had no power over him. His faithfulness was such that he ended up dying in a cross. The death of the innocent one unmasked the forces of death, exposing them in public defeat (Colossians 2:15).

This particular understanding of the faith leads me, then, to affirm Jesus' victory over sin.

....

Phil Snider

The idea that Jesus lived a life without sin was a fairly common assumption in the Christian scriptures. There are several verses that highlight this idea, and it's probably seen most clearly in Hebrews 4:15: "For we do not have a high priest [Jesus Christ] who is unable to sympathize with our weaknesses, but we have one who in every respect has been tested as we are, yet without sin."

Believing that Jesus was sinless has been very important for Christians. It implies that Jesus met the requirements necessary to be an unblemished lamb fit for sacrifice. Though I understand the reasons why many Christians interpret Jesus' death as a sacrifice for our sins, I don't think this is a helpful doctrine (mostly because it implies that God can only save us through violence).

To be honest, if I found out that Jesus told some white lies and used some foul language, it wouldn't bother me very much. I'm perfectly fine with the idea that Jesus could've had a girlfriend or been married, even though the historical likelihood of that is very minimal. In the end, what draws me toward Jesus is the vision he proclaimed as well as his courage to stand true to his convictions even in the face of death. This is what has transformed my own life, and it's one of the main reasons I affirm him as the Christ.

José F. Morales Jr.

"When anyone brings from the herd or flock a fellowship offering to the LORD . . . , it must be *without defect or blemish* to be acceptable." (Leviticus 22:21, NIV)

"For you know that it was not with perishable things such as silver or gold that you were redeemed . . . but with the precious blood of Christ, a lamb *without blemish or defect*." (1 Peter 1:18–19, NIV)

"For we do not have a high priest who is unable to sympathize with our weaknesses, but we have one who has been tempted in every way, just as we are—yet was *without sin*." (Hebrew 4:15, NIV)

The defense for a sinless Jesus is indispensible if you believe that substitutionary atonement is the cornerstone of the gospel. Substitutionary atonement asserts that God's justice needed to be satisfied with a *perfect* sacrifice, so God offered his Son, a "lamb without blemish," for our sins.

I personally have some issues with this view. Nevertheless, I still believe that Jesus was sinless, but not for substitutionary reasons. (Sorry, fellow critical Christians! I guess I can't shake off my early indoctrination.)

My reason for a Christ without sin stems from my definition of "sin." There's a difference between "sin" and "sins." "Sins" (plural) means "missing the mark" or "mistakes." The sixteenth century reformer Martin Luther reminded the church that "sin" (singular) means "separation"—from God, each other, and creation (Genesis 3).

I believe that Jesus, the lamb of God, was without sin because he walked the earth in complete union with God. As John's Jesus declared, "Whoever has seen me has seen the Father" (John 14:9); and "The Father and I are one" (John 10:30).

And this sinless Jesus saves us by overcoming the separation and bringing us back in union with God. Paul declared that God "reconciled us to himself through Christ" (2 Corinthians 5:18). And Jesus prayed for us all, saying, "I ask . . . that they may all be one. As you, Father, are in me and I am in you" (John 17:20–21).

....

L. Shannon Moore

If we take what the Bible has to say at face value, then Jesus did live without sin. The New Testament says explicitly that Jesus was without sin. But here's the deal: What is sin? If we want to get nitpicky about it then Jesus may not have been as perfect as we imagined.

Looking at the laws of Moses, Jesus walks on thin ice. He does not obey the command to be fruitful and multiply. He entices James and John to leave their father's fishing enterprise *and* he ignores his own mother when she wants to speak to him, thus breaking the command to honor our parents. Jesus allows his disciples to pluck grain on the Sabbath. He, arguably, performs magic tricks (we call them miracles, but seriously—turning water into wine doesn't exactly serve humanity's greatest needs).

Even if we step outside of the Jewish laws, Jesus doesn't always act like a perfect person should. He is mean to a woman who asks him to heal her daughter, basically calling her a dog. He even contradicts his own teaching against being angry when he drives those who are conducting business in the Temple out into the streets.

If these examples seem silly, think about how often we judge others similarly. Only God, who knows our hearts and intentions, can determine with certainty what sin is. We only need to know that it is this same God who forgives us as well.

• • • • • •

Scriptural References

Genesis 1:28; 3; Exodus 3:14; 20:12; Leviticus 22; Deuteronomy 18:10; Isaiah 53:9; Matthew 4:21–22; 5:21; Mark 3:31; 7:25–30; 10:17–18; Luke 6:1–15; John 2:1–11, 13–16; 10:22–30; 14:5–14; 17:20–26; 2 Corinthians 5:21; Hebrews 4:14–16; 1 Peter 1:13–25; 2:22; 1 John 1:8–10; 3:5

Suggested Additional Sources for Reading

- Marcus Borg, *Jesus: Uncovering the Life, Teachings, and Relevance of a Religious Revolutionary* (HarperSanFrancisco, 2006).

- Mark Dever, "Nothing But the Blood," *Christianity Today*, May 2006. http://www.christianitytoday.com/ct/2006/may/9.29.html.

- Stanley J. Grenz, "Sin: The Destruction of Community," in *Theology for the Community of God* (Eerdmans, 2000).

- William C. Placher, "How Does Jesus Save?," *Christian Century*, June 2, 2009. http://findarticles.com/p/articles/mi_m1058/is_11_126/ai _n32106634.

- Peter K. Stevenson and Stephen I. Wright, *Preaching the Atonement* (T & T Clark, 2005).

- Thomas F. Torrance, *Atonement: The Person and Work of Christ* (IVP Academic, 2009).

Suggested Questions for Further Discussion/Thought

1. What is your definition of sin? Does it have more to do with the behavior of individuals (i.e., telling a lie, rushing to war, etc.) or the condition that human beings find themselves in (i.e., the recognition that human beings are flawed and inevitably make mistakes)?

2. Is God the only one who can "determine with certainty what sin is"?

3. Do you consider the examples of Jesus' behavior that the writer suggested to be sins? Why or why not?

4. Have you ever thought about the dynamics of systemic sin (i.e., the ways that social structures benefit some people and hurt other people)? How might systemic sin diminish God's dreams for all creation?

5. How important is the notion of a sinless Christ for you? Why?

6. What's Jesus' role in salvation? And what does "salvation" mean to you?

7. What is the difference between "magic" and "miracle?"

Why did Jesus cry out "My God, my God, why have you forsaken me?" from the cross? Did God really abandon him? If so, doesn't this mean that Jesus wasn't actually God?

....
David Lose

Early in its history, the Christian church realized it had four accounts of Jesus that, while similar in many respects, were also quite different in others. In response, some favored choosing one gospel—a guy named Marcion wanted to keep Luke and get rid of the rest. Others wanted to blend them together—a guy named Tatian harmonized them into one seamless volume that was pretty popular for about two hundred years. Eventually, however, the church decided that we actually got a richer, *truer* picture of Jesus by having four distinct perspectives. Think of a complex sculpture and how you will see and appreciate it differently depending on where you're standing.

The diversity and richness of the four gospel witnesses is nowhere more evident than in their distinct portrayals of Jesus' passion. John's Jesus is strong—he has no second thoughts in the garden and doesn't need anyone to carry his cross (19:17). Luke's Jesus is reliably compassionate and full of healing—only Luke tells us, for instance, that on the eve of the crucifixion, when one of the disciples cuts off the ear of the high priest's slave, Jesus pauses to heal the slave (22:51).

What's called Jesus' "cry of dereliction" occurs in Mark and Matthew. Indeed, it is the only "word from the cross" in these two accounts and indicates how fully human Jesus is and how completely he identifies with us. Some have said that because Jesus' prayer is taken from Psalm 22, it actually conveys Jesus' continued fidelity and confidence. But I suspect that Mark and Matthew were more interested in confessing to Christians who have themselves at times felt abandoned by God that they have a Lord and Savior that knows the depths of our sorrows and struggles . . . and understands them.

....
Phil Snider

According to G. K. Chesterton, Jesus' words on the cross testify that Christianity is the only religion in which God, for an instant, became an atheist. Similar religious thinkers have taken this a step further by saying that the most radical implication of the doctrine of the incarnation (the belief that God became human) is that, upon the death of Christ, God dies. This perspective not only takes the incarnation quite seriously but also leads to the conclusion that Christianity is a properly atheistic religion.

This may sound absurd, but the idea behind such thinking is summarized by twentieth-century theologian Dietrich Bonhoeffer: "God lets himself be pushed out of the world on to the cross. He is weak and powerless in the world, and that is precisely the way, the only way, in which he is with us and helps us . . . Christ helps us, not by virtue of his omnipotence, but by virtue of his weakness and suffering." Here, the "God who is with us is the God who forsakes us . . . Before God and with God we live without God."[7]

Perhaps the subversive kernel of Christianity is that God doesn't run the world but instead dies to the world. This in turn allows human beings to exert radical freedom and responsibility for the sake of the world. After all, when human beings leave it to some "big other" to fix everything, they neglect the radical freedom and responsibility that God has already given them. Thus it can be said that God's death is necessary in order for God's transformative work to begin.

. . . .

Chris Haw

A. It partly depends on which gospel you are drawing from. Given my answer on the gospels, it should come as no surprise that John does not write this into his story.

The literary device here is a *remez*, which hints at a larger meaning by using a small citation. So the reader is supposed to *read all of Psalm 22* as a background here. Chesterton sees that this is the one moment when even God became an atheist—and depending on how deep your philosophy can go, this is either rhetorical flourish, a citation of an otherwise hopeful Psalm, or profound engagement with the absence of God.

We all can admit that Jesus' hopefulness and enchantment with the world is at least more sublime and clear than the hopes of atheism. But Jesus' capacity for despair, atheism, and disenchantment also appears to me as more courageous and aggressive than the so-called new atheism—a philosophy that Eugene McCarraher considers, on some points, a mere acquiescence to the nihilism of global capitalism. After all, it is one thing to say "life is meaningless" or "God is dead" from a well-funded professor seat or through overwrought existentialist self-pity; it is another to declare it while being tortured to death when standing up for goodness and justice.

Like I said previously, the gospels appear to necessitate some kind of indirect relationship with God—like, being a "son" or "sent by" or "united with." It does not seem unreasonable therefore to imagine Jesus feeling this "sent" degrading into a confused "abandoned," especially in a moment of agonizing torture.

. . . .
Sherri Emmons

Jesus' cry on the cross is one of the most gut-wrenching parts of the Bible, and one of the most profound proofs of his humanity. He felt the same pain we feel and had the same doubts. This passage is a big part of the reason I stay in the Christian church because I know that Christ understands my pains, my mistakes, and my doubts. And if Jesus is a part of God, then God understands, too.

But of course God did not abandon Jesus, any more than God abandons us when we are experiencing pain and loss. Life always involves pain and loss, that's how we grow as human beings. And God is with us in our pain, through the love that we show to one another in bad times, following Jesus' example.

. . . .
Jarrod McKenna

Wrenching against his tearing flesh to raise his chest for air, the breath that created the world now gasps under the brutality of good creation corrupted. Crowned only with the thorns of our shame, dressed only in the dignity that could not be gambled away, this strange naked flame burns alone on this desert bush between two failed revolutionaries.

As deep calls to deep, so Eloi cries to Eloi, "*Lama sabachthani*!" into the darkening silence of the sky. Piercing doubt sung out faithfully in the pain-riddled poetry of the twenty-second Psalm, hope and horror wrestle in the excruciating cries of a suffering God. Out of the same lamenting lips Jesus calls from the misery of our slavery and cries simultaneously God's scandalous response. The presence is only felt in the ground-shaking absence.

Flowing from the true temple's hands, feet, and side is the defeat of evil, the end of exile, the forgiveness of sins, and the *shekinah* glory that will flood the earth with the presence of peace. Women weep from a distance as God is in Christ reconciling the world to himself. Yet it seems that God is dead to God. How strange a coronation that crowns the returning King with crucifixion, announcing that the meek one has inherited the earth and reigns not with a sword but as the Suffering Servant of all.

Why did Jesus cry out "My God, my God, why have you forsaken me?" Such questions are best asked from awe-filled silence of contemplation from where we can see why the centurion in terrified wonder would whisper the words, "Surely, this man was the Son of God."

• • • • • •

Scriptural References

Psalm 22; Isaiah 53; Matthew 27:27–56; Mark 15:16–41, 33–34;
1 Corinthians 1:18–31; 2:2; 2 Corinthians 5:16–21

Suggested Additional Sources for Reading

- David Lose, *Making Sense of Scripture* (Augsburg Fortress Press, 2009).
- Enter the Bible: http://www.enterthebible.org.
- G. K. Chesterton, *Orthodoxy* (John Lane, 1909).
- Dietrich Bonhoeffer, *Letters and Papers from Prison* (Touchstone, 1997).
- Adam Kotsko, *Žižek and Theology* (T & T Clark, 2008).
- John Caputo and Gianni Vattimo, *After the Death of God* (Columbia Univ. Press, 2007).
- N. T. Wright, *Following Jesus: Biblical Reflections on Discipleship* (Eerdmans, 1995).
- Lee C. Camp, *Mere Discipleship* (Brazos Press, 2003).
- Brad Jersak and Michael Hardin, *Stricken by God?: Nonviolent Identification and the Victory of Christ* (Eerdmans, 2007).
- Martin Scorsese, director, *The Last Temptation of Christ* (Universal Films, 1988).
- Marcus J. Borg and John Dominic Crossan, *The Last Week: A Day-by-Day Account of Jesus' Final Week in Jerusalem* (HarperOne, 2006).

Suggested Questions for Further Discussion/Thought

1. Of what value is it to know that however abandoned you may feel, Jesus has also felt that way and understands?
2. If "Christ helps us, not by virtue of his omnipotence, but by virtue of his weakness and suffering" (as Bonhoeffer suggests), do you think Christ's influence on your life becomes less important or more important?
3. Can you think of times when people have used Christian beliefs as an excuse not to care for the world? Name some examples.
4. Have you ever been moved to tears by the horrific beauty of a love that would undergo the cross?

Aren't Jesus' miracles similar to other healings and miracles recorded outside the Jewish and Christian tradition?

....
Brandon Gilvin

Absolutely. The ancient Near East was full of stories of magicians and miracle workers, many Jewish, and many served as antecedents for the stories of Jesus. Prophets such as Elisha (2 Kings) and Isaiah performed a number of acts that Jesus' miracles evoke.

Stories of miracles by Jesus' contemporaries such as Honi the Circle Drawer also continue to draw attention from historical-Jesus scholars.

And of course, similar healing stories, miracles, and miraculous births are attributed to other religious figures (human and divine) from other traditions.

Such stories have a variety of meanings within the contexts of the communities that teach them. From my perspective, it is less important to compare stories of traditions, as if we could judge which one is the most historically accurate, than it is for us to be able to ask what the stories of Jesus healing others has to say for us as twenty-first century Christians. Whether or not Jesus was a first century magician or a Hippocratic practitioner is not as much as a concern for me—but how we follow Jesus' example by working for sustainable health, nutrition, HIV and AIDS prevention, and other important issues in struggling communities is.

....
Mark Van Steenwyk

There have always been stories of wonder workers. And while there were certainly folks claiming miraculous powers wandering around the Roman Empire around the time of Jesus, it wasn't all that common. Nevertheless, popular perception tends to reflect the sensibilities of Monty Python's *The Life of Brian* where there seemed to be a messiah around every corner.

But that wasn't really the case. Respected scholar Raymond E. Brown wrote, "One should be wary of the claim that Jesus was portrayed like the many other miracle-working teachers, Jewish and pagan, of his era. The idea that such a figure was a commonplace in the 1st century is largely a fiction. Jesus is remembered as combining teaching with miracles intimately related to his teaching and that combination may be unique."[10]

Some folks claimed to do miracles. Most of these folks did it for personal profit—to wow the crowds. And there were certainly many spiritual teachers. But Jesus is largely unique in the way that he combined his miracles with his message. He didn't do miracles so that the crowds could be amazed. Rather he did acts of power to liberate people from oppression. His miracles were intentional acts of service and liberation. In his miracles, he fed the hungry. He gave sight to the blind. He cast demons out of the oppressed. He was, in everything he said and did, a liberator.

....

Peter J. Walker

A. Yes. Miracles have occurred in cultures and religions throughout history (as theological "proof," miracles only make a case for universalism more compelling). The church often argues that its truth relies on the historical anomaly of Christ, using miracles as key evidence. That's why things like the Zeitgeist videos on YouTube go viral so quickly and cause so much damage: We talk about how Jesus is wholly unique among world religions, and then what? Hope someone doesn't Google *Horus*, *Krishna*, or *Siddhārtha Gautama*?

C. S. Lewis argued that Christianity's profound difference is in its *historical* reality: that all religions echo a similar metanarrative but only one is the "true myth," the rest are like reflections in a mirror. I'm not sure I would even go that far. When I married my wife, I chose to stop playing "what if" about other beautiful women. I made a choice to give myself to her and to trust her based on who I knew her to be—*not* based on a belief that no other women existed. Have I stopped finding other women attractive? Do I believe she is the only person in the world I could ever be happy with? I won't play naive. But we *know* each other, and we have committed to exclusively love one another.

I have committed to loving Christ, not because I think he is my only available option or because I think his *miracles* uniquely prove his truth or even because I find other religions less compelling. I remain in this relationship because I have the audacity to believe I *know* Christ. Rather than passive belief, faith is a miracle I choose to participate in.

....

Phil Snider

A. While the short answer to this question is yes, it's important to keep in mind that the people who wrote the gospels used the miracle stories about Jesus in order to talk about the way their lives changed as a result of following Jesus. One of the coolest things about these stories is the way they function on several different levels at once, both literally and figuratively.

For instance, Mark's gospel describes two stories that each feature Jesus restoring the sight of a blind man (Mark 8:22–26 and 10:46–52). Close readers of Mark will notice these stories working together as a frame that surrounds Jesus' journey to Jerusalem, the place where Jesus ultimately confronts the powers that be and loses his life as a result. By framing Jesus' journey with these stories, part of what Mark tells us is that if we have the courage to follow Jesus all the way to Jerusalem—by joining Jesus in order to confront oppressive powers that be, no matter the cost—then we too will have our sight restored.

Just as the earliest followers of Jesus experienced transformation when they confronted the powers that be, no matter the cost, the same can be said of modern day heroes like Martin Luther King Jr. and Oscar Romero. When they stood up to the powers that be on behalf of the oppressed—even though they ultimately lost their own lives as a result—we affirm that (1) they are representative of those who see most clearly and (2) if we follow Jesus the same way, we just might have our sight restored as well.

· · · · · ·

Scriptural References

2 Kings; Isaiah; Mark 8:11–12, 22–26, 27–30; 10:46–52; Luke 4:14–21; 5:14

Suggested Additional Sources for Reading

- David Rhoads, *Mark as Story* (Augsburg Fortress Press, 1999).
- Marcus Borg and John Dominic Crossan, *The Last Week: What the Gospels Really Teach about Jesus's Final Days in Jerusalem* (HarperOne, 2006).
- Raymond E. Brown, *An Introduction to New Testament Christology* (Paulist Press, 1994).
- Robert Funk, *The Acts of Jesus* (Polebridge Press, 1998).
- Graham Twelftree, *Jesus the Miracle Worker* (IVP Academic, 1999).
- *Wikipedia*, s.v. "Miracles of Jesus," http://en.wikipedia.org/wiki/Miracles_of_Jesus#List_of_miracles_in_the_four_Gospels.
- *Wikipedia*, s.v. "Jesus in Comparative Mythology," http://en.wikipedia.org/wiki/Jesus_Christ_in_comparative_mythology.
- C. S. Lewis, *Mere Christianity* (Macmillan, 1952).
- C. S. Lewis, *Out of the Silent Planet* (Macmillan, 1946).
- Peter Joseph, director, *Zeitgeist: Moving Forward* (Gentle Machine, 2011). DVD available at http://www.zeitgeistmovie.com.

- Amy-Jill Levine, Dale C. Allison, John Dominic Crossan, eds., *The Historical Jesus in Context* (Princeton Univ. Press, 2006).
- James H. Charlesworth, *The Historical Jesus: An Essential Guide* (Abingdon Press, 2008).

Suggested Questions for Further Discussion/Thought

1. What would it mean if there were other miracle workers in Jesus' day?
2. Is it important to believe that Jesus was actually able to do miracles?
3. Do I need miracles to believe?
4. Can I believe in what I have not seen?
5. Does my religious faith depend on its exclusive truth?
6. Are miracles in other religions from the same God, or are they dangerous illusions?
7. Consider the theological symbolism at work in stories about Jesus turning water into wine, multiplying the loaves and fishes, walking on water, and so on. How does this affect the meaning of each story?

When Jesus participates in the Last Supper, doesn't that mean he's eating his own body and drinking his own blood?

Becky Garrison

Christians differ widely as to how they interpret the Last Supper, ranging from transubstantiation—where the bread and wine become the body and blood of Christ—to a memorial that pays homage to Jesus' last night on earth. For liturgically minded Christians (Catholic, Orthodox, Anglican, Lutheran), the ritual of receiving the body and blood of Christ becomes a sacrament, a term that means "the outward expression of an inward act."

Most Protestants tend to place their emphasis on preaching, so one might find communion administered anywhere from biweekly to not at all. Regardless of the emphasis a given denomination places on this ritualistic act, no one in his or her right mind would call Christ a cannibal. That's just disgusting.

Mark Van Steenwyk

At the Last Supper, Jesus told his disciples that the bread and wine they were eating and drinking were his body and blood. Catholics traditionally believe that when you eat the bread and wine at mass, you're actually eating the flesh and blood of Jesus. Since the Last Supper was the first communion, or eucharist, I'd imagine that Jesus eating bread and drinking wine with his disciples poses an odd question: Did Jesus eat himself at the Last Supper?

Personally, since I am not a Catholic, I'm not confronted with the question of cannibalism. I believe that communion is, for the most part, symbolic. I think Jesus was engaging in a bit of performance art—telling his disciples that he was about to be killed and that his disciples should partake of a similar sort of death. In other words, this is a vivid way of telling his followers that they should "take up their crosses" and be willing to lay down their lives for the movement.

So when it comes to the question of cannibalism, I'm off the hook. However, I believe that Christ is indeed present in a flesh-and-blood way when we share communion with one another—but that is because we, the followers of Jesus Christ, are his body and blood. He is present in us whenever we break bread together in his name. And so, I suppose, if we were to eat each other, it would count as a double dose of cannibalism!

....

Sherri Emmons

A. OK, first . . . ewww! This is what happens when we take the Bible literally, and it's why so many people today get turned off by the church. Jesus broke bread and poured wine and passed them to his friends and said, "Take, eat, this is my body, this is my blood." Did any of his disciples gag? Did they refuse to take the elements? No, because they understood that Jesus was using metaphors.

We can understand it the same way when Jesus says in Matthew 13:31, "The kingdom of heaven is like a mustard seed that someone took and sowed in his field." Is the kingdom of heaven really like a mustard seed? If we eat mustard, are we devouring the kingdom of heaven? Of course not.

Jesus taught his followers using stories and images that they could understand—he was the shepherd tending his flock; he was the bridegroom and the church, his bride. We accept these metaphors for what they are. So why do we get hung up on the bread and wine as body and blood?

• • • • • •

Scriptural References

Matthew 26; Mark 14; Luke 22; John 13

Suggested Additional Sources for Reading

- Henri Nouwen, *Can You Drink the Cup?* (Ave Maria Press, 1996).
- Sara Miles, *Take This Bread: A Radical Conversion* (Ballantine, 2008).
- John H. Armstrong, ed., *Understanding Four Views on the Lord's Supper* (Zondervan, 2007).
- Ben Witherington III, *Making a Meal of It: Rethinking the Theology of the Lord's Supper* (Baylor Univ. Press, 2008).
- Martin E. Marty, *The Lord's Supper* (Augsburg Fortress Press, 1964).

Suggested Questions for Further Discussion/Thought

1. What does it mean for you to receive the body and blood of Jesus Christ?
2. Do you think eating communion is important?
3. Why do you think Jesus made a point of eating a meal with his disciples before he was executed?

Did Jesus understand himself to be God, like God, in line with God, or something else? Did he understand this from birth? If not, then when did he begin to understand it and how?

Becky Garrison

Now we come to one of those questions that has caused way too many faith fistfights. In a nutshell, we can't answer that question definitively. According to the gospel of John, Jesus knew he was God from the beginning of time. Matthew and Mark cite the revelation of Jesus as the Messiah at the moment when he was baptized by John, while Luke points to the beginning when the boy Jesus was hanging out, doing his Father's business.

But one thing is clear—by the time Jesus set out for Jerusalem, he knew without a doubt that his kingdom was not of this world and that he was going to be crucified before rising from the dead.

R. M. Keelan Downton

If you start from a belief that Jesus came to convey a set of facts, it's pretty puzzling that there's not a checklist somewhere. If the purpose of reading the gospels is to piece together such a checklist, it is immensely important that Jesus have access to the complete knowledge of God (omniscience, if you want the jargon)—probably from puberty but at least from the beginning of his public ministry.

You need to be able to trust that each incident and phrase was carefully planned to communicate some part of that total knowledge, not the result of Jesus struggling like us to make decisions in a world of uncertain outcomes. But this makes Jesus otherworldly and disconnected from the everyday problems of life in a way that is not supported by the gospel narratives.

If, on the other hand, you start from an assertion that Jesus came to proclaim and enact the true order of the world, the first question is not "how did Jesus think about himself?" but "does Jesus reveal God?" The complete answer to this second question can only be seen from the other side of the resurrection: the way that Jesus reveals God demonstrates that Jesus, as Messiah and Christ, must be God.

L. Shannon Moore

I'll answer this backward. Based on the only biblical account pertaining to Jesus' boyhood, I think he always knew he had a special purpose. Separated from his parents, and later found in the temple having a discussion with the teachers, Jesus' reply in Luke 2 to his mother's scolding is, "I must be in my Father's house."

I don't think, however, that Jesus knew the importance of what God had in store for him until his baptism. In three books of the Bible, we read that after Jesus is baptized, the heavens open, the Spirit of God descends upon him, and a voice from heaven (presumably God's) declares him to be the "beloved Son." Talk about pressure.

And so it seems that throughout the gospels, Jesus sees himself as just that—God's beloved Son, sent to help people better understand God by forgiving their sins, healing the sick, and advocating justice for the poor. He prayed *to* God and preached *about* God, but did not consider himself to *be* God.

One of the main reasons that people attribute divinity to Jesus is because of the miracles that he performed. But Jesus kind of explains this in Matthew 17 when he says, "If you have faith and do not doubt . . . if you say to this mountain, 'Be lifted up and thrown into the sea,' it will be done." And that's the way I see it—Jesus saw himself as a human, sent from God, and gifted with the ability to do extraordinary things because *he did not doubt*.

Chris Haw

It depends on which gospel you ask. The synoptic gospels (Matthew, Mark, Luke) all share a type of Jesus—no doubt with some variations—whose humanity is more emphasized than the Jesus in John. While the synoptics certainly have their colors of divinity mixed in, John's Jesus easily foretells events, can see beyond where his body is, and seems in charge of even his own arrest and death.

But even the highest Johannine proclamations from Jesus' mouth still involve some kind of mediation and indirection. John Robinson, in *Honest to God*, puts it something like this: "Jesus never says directly, 'I am God.' Rather, everything has some kind of differentiation, like 'if you have seen me, you have seen God' or 'I and the Father are One,' or 'the Father sent me,' etc." Jesus doesn't say, "I am the Father" rather he is sent from the Father, has seen him, is united with him, and so on.

Perhaps even more interestingly, what do we even mean by "God"? N. T. Wright also takes this up this quite well in his book *Jesus and the Victory of God* by asking what the word *God* meant, particularly in Jesus' day. Jesus is a fantastic instance to ask, "[J]udging from him, what is God and what is humanity?" For, in this person, we see both redefined.

"God," whatever that means, is something or someone who would love us, forgive us for our murderous evils, teach us, heal us, and submit to being crucified by us. And a "human," whatever that means, is someone who can live in union with God or reveal the very being of God.

· ·

Amy Reeder Worley

A. I was raised in a southern, fundamentalist Christian church and taught that Jesus is both *the Son of* God and *is* God. When I asked how Jesus could be human *and* God, I got an unsatisfying shtick about a house—God was a house and Jesus was a room in that house. They were the same but different. That metaphor only frustrated me.

I spent years divorced from Christianity because I could not intellectually conceive of Jesus' relationship to God in this way. Surprisingly it was my foray into Buddhism and Yoga that motivated me to rethink the "God language" I learned as a child.

Jesus articulates how he viewed himself in relation to God in Luke. Jesus, quoting Isaiah, says, "The spirit of the Lord is *on me*, because he *has anointed* me to preach good news to the poor. He has sent me to proclaim freedom for the prisoners, and recovery of sight for the blind, and to set the oppressed free" (Luke 4:18, NIV).

As a child, I had been told Jesus' divinity was like a math problem. Divine = God. Thus Human Jesus + Divinity = God. But divine also means "of, relating to, emanating from, or being the expression of" God. My practice of Yoga taught that spiritual seekers strive to "yoke" or "bring together" humankind and God. Informed by my yogic and Buddhist reading, I came to understand that Jesus viewed himself as being *anointed by* God—*that is*, yoked with the sacred.

Through prayer, submission, and devaluing material things (also Buddhist concepts) Jesus, acting *of* or *in* God, worked for justice and sought to heal those "blind" to God's ways. The hope in this Christology is that by following the way of Jesus we too can yoke ourselves with the sacred.

● ● ● ● ● ●

Scriptural References

Matthew 3:16–17; Mark 1:10–11; 6:45; Luke 2:41–52; 3:21–22; 4:18; 21:21; 22:42; John 1:1–5; Acts 17:28

Suggested Additional Sources for Reading

- Marcus Borg and N. T. Wright, *Meaning of Jesus: Two Visions* (HarperOne, 2007).
- Patanjali, *The Yoga Sutras*, trans. Edwin F. Bryant (North Point Press, 2009).
- Thich Nat Hanh, *Living Buddha, Living Christ* (Riverhead, 1995).
- Marcus Borg, *Jesus and Buddha: The Parallel Sayings* (Ulysses Press, 1997).
- Paul Knitter, *Without Buddha I Could Not Be a Christian* (Oneworld, 2009).
- Thomas Merton, *New Seeds of Contemplation* (New Directions, 1961).
- John A. T. Robinson, *Honest to God* (SCM, 1963).
- N. T. Wright, *The Challenge of Jesus* (InterVarsity Press, 1999), especially chapter 5.

Suggested Questions for Further Discussion/Thought

1. Why can't the gospel writers come to a consensus regarding the moment Jesus of Nazareth knew he was Christ, the Messiah, and Son of God?
2. Is it important to believe that Jesus is God?
3. Could you be a Christian if you knew without a doubt that Jesus was not divine?
4. Are there any God terms that you may need to rethink or redefine?
5. Do you believe that God is "out there" somewhere, as opposed to a force within and of the world?
6. What can you discern in the Bible about the early churches' view of Jesus' relationship to God? How is it similar or different from your view?

If Jesus could resurrect people, why didn't he do it more often?

Brandon Gilvin

A. The first thing to remember is that resurrection is not the same thing as resuscitation.

To resuscitate a body is to revive it—whether the cause is medical or miracle, one who is physically dead regains breath, mental capacity, and use of his or her faculties.

Resurrection is something else. The early disciples experienced Jesus' presence following his death in very powerful, "real" ways. Whether or not the resurrection was the actual resuscitation of Jesus' body can never be historically verified.

The resurrection of Jesus took on many meanings for the early Jesus movement—the great love of God for humanity and God's sovereignty over death and the political forces of death. Resurrection is more of a theological concept than a physical act.

For contemporary Christians, to say we believe in the resurrection does not necessarily mean that we believe that rotting human bodies can be reanimated (either now or in the first century), but our shared conviction that despite the realities of death, sickness, poverty, and oppression there is always hope for healing, health, and reconciliation and that it is core to Christian practice to help make such hope reality.

The stories of Jesus (and the apostles in Acts) performing resurrections point readers to choose peace in the face of violence, hope in the face of despair, and life in the face of death.

Christian Piatt

A. Stories of healing and raising the dead in scripture seem to raise more questions than they answer. And the raising of Lazarus in the gospel of John is perhaps the best known of these.

Why did Jesus pick Lazarus? Why not someone else, perhaps an innocent child? Why did he let Lazarus die in the first place? Why not intervene before he died? And is it some kind of cruel joke that Lazarus ultimately will have to die all over again? If you think about it, there's nothing that ever said those fed by Jesus never hungered again, or those healed of disease never got sick after that.

So are these miracles, such as the one involving Lazarus, just a selfish demonstration of power by Jesus? Was he showing favoritism? Did he care less about those he didn't save from suffering?

It helps to consider *why* the miracle stories are included throughout the gospels, namely to point in a particular direction where Jesus is leading throughout his ministry. Considered from a literary perspective, the story of Lazarus' resurrection parallels that of Jesus' resurrection in a number of ways. And by including this toward the end of Jesus' ministry on earth, the author is offering a foreshadowing of the death-conquering power expressed by Christ's love for humanity.

Jesus acknowledged that suffering was an inevitable byproduct of physical life. But the miracle stories provide at least small windows through which we can see a way out of the suffering, toward an existence in perfect communion with God, casting aside the struggles and hardships of this world, like so many rags left behind by Lazarus at the tomb.

That is the *real* life-giving message of the gospels.

• • • • • • • • • • • • •

Joan Ball

This is such an "if I were God, this is how I would do it" kind of question. Forget why Jesus didn't resurrect people more often. Why is there death at all? Why hunger? Why do we get thirsty? Wouldn't it have been better to design the human body without the need for fuel and eliminate the need for food and drink altogether? Why is the sky blue? Are we there yet?

Eventually our questions about God are so similar to those children ask about the world around them that, if we are humble, we will begin to see that part of having faith in God is recognizing that there are questions for which we will never have answers. His ways are not our ways, which makes understanding God's thoughts challenging, if not impossible, for us. We are operating on a different set of assumptions and, in our arrogance, we frequently attempt to have God shift to our assumptions rather than conforming ourselves to God's.

• • • • • •

Scriptural References

Isaiah 55:8–9; Mark 16:1–8; John 11:1–46; Acts 9:36–43; Philippians 2:6–11; Colossians

Suggested Additional Sources for Reading

- J. N. D. Kelly, *Early Christian Doctrines* (A. & C. Black, 1958).
- Henry Chadwick, *The Early Church* (Hodder & Stoughton, 1968).
- Justo Gonzalez, *The Story of Christianity*, vol. 1 (HarperOne, 2010).
- Karen Armstrong, *A History of God* (Ballantine, 1994).
- Esther de Waal, *Living with Contradiction: An Introduction to Benedictine Spirituality* (Morehouse, 1998).
- Emmet Fox, *The Sermon on the Mount* (HarperOne, 1989).

Suggested Questions for Further Discussion/Thought

1. Which is more important: the actual miracles Jesus was said to have performed or the message they seem to convey?
2. What do you believe was the main reason for resurrections performed in scripture?

Was Jesus a pacifist?

Jarrod McKenna

A. No.
Jesus did not come to bring peace but a sword. And we as disciples must wield the same sword Jesus brings, and no other.

The question is, what is this sword?

What is this sword that heals rather than harms enemies?

What is this sword that never collaborates or mirrors the powers, thereby exposing their addiction to violence?

What is this sword that prophetically turns over tables of idolatry and injustice in a judgment that does not harm, hurt, coerce, or kill anyone?

What is this fire that is ablaze with the very presence of I Am in response to the cries of the oppressed, this fire that does not destroy the bush in which it burns?

What is this power that is ablaze on the cross, sucking the oxygen of injustice and violence from creation, which then causes a cosmic backdraft in the resurrection, setting the world alight with the love that conquers death?

This sword of Christ is something far more dangerous and dynamic than a philosophy of an ideal, static, passive peace read back onto the life of Christ. Martin Luther King Jr. would insist it is a peace that "is not the absence of tension but the presence of justice." It is the mystery our Lord Jesus embodies, enabling a new world where what we once wasted on bombs is now used to feed the hungry.

Jesus is no pacifist. He is YHWH's nonviolent Suffering Servant whose grace calls us to share in his tears over what would make for peace, whose Spirit empowers us to take up the sword of nonviolence as our only weapon in witness to the victory Christ has won.

Chris Haw

A. The Temple cleansing would seem to imply, "no." But we must be careful to note here how he did not kill (or even, it seems, harm) anybody in this well-documented incident. And the early Jesus followers seem to have taken no inspiration from this story as a type of action to imitate, as we have no documentation of *early* Christians carrying swords or rioting after Jesus' famous "Put your sword back into its place; for all who take the sword will perish by the sword" (Matthew 26:52).

In sum, nothing in the canon contradicts Jesus' oft-ignored teaching, "Love your enemies." And seeing as he gives three concrete examples of how to do so in practice, I do not think he meant this metaphorically, or as Luther pontificated—that one can kill one's enemy and love them at the same time.

In an etymologically strict sense, it is probably beneficial to think that Jesus' politics did involve attempts to "pacify" one's enemy. Walking an extra mile with the demanding officer is just one attempt at pacification. Granted, his speaking truth to his accusers ("why did you hit me?") could have perhaps enflamed their hatred—though I am inclined to think of the enflaming as the fault of the violent, not the lamb.

R. M. Keelan Downton

It is clear that Jesus is doing something different when he tells his disciples to respond to being slapped, robbed, or forced to work with a creative response that would evoke shame or other complications for the abuser. It is less clear whether Jesus ever intended this to be scaled up to the level of nation-state (which, of course, hadn't been invented, but like empire, requires significant levels of violence to maintain).

Discussions of whether Jesus is a pacifist get muddled by confusion about the meaning of "violence." I once heard a speaker ask, "How can we reject violence as a means of resisting capitalism? I mean, even Jesus used violence against bankers!" This misses a critical distinction.

To be pacifist means to reject the use of deadly force as a legitimate means of resolving disputes—it does not mean allowing injustice to continue without challenge. It does not mean that those who wish to do violence cannot be constrained legally, economically, or even physically.

The space between inaction and murder is precisely where we see Jesus operating in his dealings with the Roman Empire and the Temple entrepreneurs. Even at the end of Revelation (which some people read as a Rambo-esque return) it is important to remember that the "sword" comes from Jesus' mouth and the blood is Jesus' own.

Tripp Fuller

It is perfectly clear that Jesus was against violence and war as means of setting things right. He told his disciples to turn the other cheek, not to resist an evildoer, to pray for their enemies, and then forgave his own enemies from the cross.

But does this make him a pacifist? Would he be one today in our historical situation? Most conversations around this topic quickly devolve into attempts to justify some act of violence (protecting an innocent child) or moral war (putting an end to genocide), yet this misses the larger point of Jesus' embodied teaching. The reason Jesus and God's kingdom reject violence is not because it can't bring about a victory, but because an act of violence leads to a victor who is also a violator of their victims.

Eventually power shifts and the previous victims feel justified in becoming the new violent victors. God's kingdom's way, embodied by Jesus and taught to the disciples, is a way that does not reach victory by building crosses but by bearing them. The ultimate victory of God is a victory for all because through the resurrection, God becomes *victor* by becoming the *victim.*

In doing so God identifies and shares in the suffering of the world and charts a path for reconciliation, even for the violators. This larger perspective reframes the nature of Jesus' "pacifism," asking his followers today not to become passively peaceful but active peacemakers and ambassadors of God's reconciliation.

• • • • • •

Scriptural References

Matthew 5:38–48; 2 Corinthians 5:16–21

Suggested Additional Sources for Reading

- John Yoder, *The Politics of Jesus: Vicit Agnus Noster* (Eerdmans, 1972).
- John Yoder, "Peace Without Eschatology; or, If Christ is Truly Lord" in *The Original Revolution: Essays on Christian Pacifism* (Herald Press, 1972).
- André Trocmé, *Jesus and the Nonviolent Revolution* (Herald Press, 1973).
- Walter Wink, *Jesus and Nonviolence: A Third Way* (Fortress Press, 2003).

Suggested Questions for Further Discussion/Thought

1. Do you think the story of Jesus and the money changers in the temple is an example of him being violent? Why or why not?
2. Is there ever a time when violence is justified?
3. Is the violent act of Jesus' crucifixion justifiable? Why or why not?

Did Jesus believe God wanted him to be crucified? If so, why did he ask God, "My Father, if it is possible, let this cup pass from me" in the garden of Gethsemane?

Jarrod McKenna

There is a stunning image from the Tiananmen Square uprising in 1989. A lone student places himself in front of the rolling war machines of one of the world's largest oppressive superpowers. Armed only with what looks like a bag and a vision of the future, he refuses to be passive and steps out, allowing the possibility of history and hope to clash over his body.

Burnt into our collective memory is this fragile symbol of democracy on a collision course with the Communist government's power. What would the night before this action be like for him? Did this student have a sense of vocation that his life would be given to open up a new reality for his people?

Our Lord Jesus is not less human than this warrior whose only weapon was unarmed truth. And Jesus didn't do less than what the student did in taking an oppressive empire. On the cross, Jesus took on all evil, and all empires, exhausting their worst in his very body and astonishingly responds with "Father, forgive them for they do not know what they are doing" (Luke 23:34).

Jesus in the garden prays what any one of us would pray for, another way other than the pain of confrontational suffering love. Jesus prays in the garden (Matthew 26:39, 42) as he taught his disciples to pray (Matthew 6:9–13) "your will be done" and in doing so goes to the cross, bringing the coming kingdom on Earth as it is in heaven. In taking upon himself the suffering that initiates the end of all suffering, Jesus does not simply do the will of God; Jesus *is* the will of God.

Joan Ball

I believe Jesus' request was a prayer for mercy. He knew the pain and suffering that lay before him, and he was willing to take it to the bitter end. Being fully human and fully divine, he engaged his humanity by engaging in prayer and petition to ask the Father if there was another way.

While modern western Christians have created a culture where questioning God is often viewed as a lack of faithfulness, Jesus was a Jew.

Questioning, negotiating, and wrestling with God was not only acceptable, it was—and still is—a critical part of the faith tradition. To cry out to the Father was in keeping with the example set by king David and the Old Testament prophets underscoring the notion that we can question God and be faithful to God in the same breath.

....

R. M. Keelan Downton

A It doesn't take any prophetic powers for a leader who is attracting large crowds with teachings that challenge the authority of both the religious and the political establishments to conclude that continuing to do so will likely result in death.

If you start from the perspective of Jesus having access to the full knowledge of God, the Gethsemane prayer is inherently confusing: Jesus knows it's important that he be crucified but asks if God could work it out some other way. From this perspective, "your will be done" is a fatalistic resignation to suffering—a perspective that has been immensely destructive in the history of the church, particularly to women.

If Jesus is only working from knowledge of the likely outcome, it means that Jesus prayed out of the same struggle we face: embodying love and justice in the face of loss and uncertainty. "Let this cup pass" is a real search for a creative solution beyond what circumstances suggest will happen. From this perspective, "your will be done" means participating in the intentions of God for the world, even when those in power oppose those intentions.

The suffering perpetuated by Roman torturers is not intended to set out suffering as an ideal, but rather serves as the radical sign that those who resist God by inflicting suffering on others cannot win. Their actions are truly horrific and yet insufficient to prevent the ultimate victory of God the gospel invites us to participate in.

....

Lee C. Camp

A The four gospels indicate a purposeful intentionality in Jesus' moving toward Jerusalem. Jesus seems quite aware that this would entail his own crucifixion. What could the prayer in the Garden mean, then? The synoptic gospels each recount Jesus' temptation experience in the wilderness at the beginning of his ministry. Many times, these temptations are understood to be a reference to the "lust of the flesh, lust of the eye, and the vain-glorious pride of life," a way of saying that Jesus was simply tempted in all points like as we are.

But more likely, the temptation accounts raise a different concern: *What sort of messiah will Jesus be?* A welfare king, who puts a car in every garage and a chicken in every pot? A religious reformer, who makes a great spectacle in the Temple and sets right matters of a proper religious cult once and for all? Or will he be a mighty emperor, ruling over all lands through imperialistic might?

From that point forward, Jesus set out to be a very different sort of messiah, one who shall save the world through suffering love. When in Mark 8, for example, Jesus teaches the twelve that his being "Son of Man" will entail abuse and mocking and death, Peter rebukes Jesus: "Do not say such a thing, Jesus! You are the Messiah, and no Messiah should face such." Jesus' response is instructive: "Get behind me, Satan." That is, Peter has voiced the same temptation Jesus faced in the wilderness: Go be a conquering messiah, not a suffering one.

Then in the final hours before the crucifixion, Jesus faces the temptation again: Must this really be the way? Is there no other? May I not call ten thousand angels to vanquish evil?

·················
David Lose

A. The testimony of the early church to Jesus—including what Jesus *knew* about his crucifixion—is both rich and varied. Jesus' prayer to "let this cup pass" is in Matthew, Mark, and Luke—called the "synoptic" (Greek for "seen together") gospels because they are the most similar. In John's gospel, by contrast, Jesus not only shows no such moment of weakness, but when Peter attempts to defend him by the sword, Jesus asks the opposite question: "Am I *not* to drink the cup that the Father has given me?" (John 18:11).

At this point, we therefore have two options: Either try to decide which of the gospel accounts was "right," or listen carefully for the distinct confession of faith that each gospel writer offers. In the case of the prayer in the synoptic gospels, two theological confessions come to the fore. First, Jesus is *like us* and so experiences these events as we might experience them. Who wouldn't be anxious regarding the impending struggle, suffering, and death the cross represents? Second, Jesus is *faithful*. Whatever human fear Jesus displays, he is nevertheless faithful to his father, to his mission, and to us. Hence his prayer continues, "[Y]et not what I want, but what you want" (Mark 14:36).

So there you have it. Jesus is really *like* us, and therefore understands the challenges and struggles we endure. And Jesus is really *for* us, committed to us enough that he would suffer and die on the cross. Not a bad set of confessions to hang on to when you, yourself, feel stretched beyond your limits.

• • • • • •

Scriptural References

Genesis 32:24–31; Matthew 6:9–13; 26:36–42; Mark 14:32–42; Luke 22:39–46

Suggested Additional Sources for Reading

- Watchman Nee, *The Normal Christian Life* (Victory Press, 1963).
- John Howard Yoder, *The Politics of Jesus* (Eerdmans, 1972).
- John Howard Yoder, *The Original Revolution* (Herald Press, 1972).
- David Lose, *Making Sense of Scripture* (Augsburg Fortress Press, 2009).
- David Lose, *Making Sense of the Christian Faith* (Augsburg Fortress Press, 2010).
- N. T. Wright, *The Challenge of Jesus* (IVP, 2011).
- Christopher D. Marshall, *Beyond Retribution* (Eerdmans, 2001).

Suggested Questions for Further Discussion/Thought

1. What does it mean to you to know that Jesus was afraid like we can be? Does it mean that Jesus understands our fears because he has experienced fear firsthand?

2. Why are verses that insist Jesus has control of his own destiny (Mark 14:35, 41; Matthew 26:55; Luke 22:14) so important?

3. Why is it important that we don't think God wills suffering but sometimes calls us to a suffering that exposes the systems that make others suffer?

4. Orthodox Christianity affirms that Jesus is fully human (as human as you) and fully divine (as divine as the Holy Spirit and the Father). Why is it that some Christians focus on one and neglect the other?

Was Jesus ever wrong? About what?

. . . .
Sherri Emmons

If we take seriously the concept that Jesus was both fully human and fully divine, then we have to accept that he made mistakes. To be human is to make mistakes. This human side of Christ is what draws me to Christianity. Knowing that Christ suffered the way we do tells me that he understands our doubts, our mistakes, and our suffering in a way no purely divine being could.

We see evidence of Jesus' humanity in his need to withdraw from the crowds, his impatience with his disciples, his anger at the moneylenders in the temple, and his pleading with God in the garden of Gethsemane. And we have one endearing example of misbehavior when Jesus as a child stays behind at the Temple after his parents have left, which certainly must have worried Mary and Joseph out of their wits. Talking with the elders was fine, but he was wrong not to tell his parents where he was.

. . . .
Joan Ball

On first blush, this question looked a lot like the question about whether Jesus had ever been sick—subject to speculation only. But as I considered the question further, the story of Jesus clearing the Temple in Jerusalem, which shows up in each of the gospels, kept coming to mind. While I am not in a position to say whether Jesus' decision to enter that courtyard and kick over the tables was right or wrong (way over my pay grade), I do know that it is a scripture that is used frequently as an excuse for unloving, aggressive behavior among Christians.

Too often we allow Christians behaving badly to call biblical principles into question, and I will not do that here. I just wonder how Jesus would feel about the holy anger and aggression that has been justified in the name of the events of that day.

R. M. Keelan Downton

This question appears to be about things that Jesus asserted or denied, but in reality it is about how the person answering positions her or himself in relation to Jesus—a question of loyalty and trust.

There are some trivial anomalies like where Jesus says he won't go up to a particular feast but then a few days later he does. But these are a distraction.

What matters is whether I choose to arrange my life to match the teachings of Jesus or not. To the extent that I do, I affirm loyalty to Jesus as Messiah/Christ who can be fully trusted. To the extent that I arrange my life in different ways, I assert that Jesus was wrong and express loyalty only to my own decision-making process.

● ● ● ● ● ●

Scriptural References

Matthew 4:13, 21:11–13; 21:12–17, 23–27; 26:36–46; Mark 11:15–19, 27–33 14:32–42; Luke 2:39–52; 19:45–48, 20:1–8; John 2:13–16

Suggested Additional Sources for Reading

- Brennan Manning, *The Furious Longing of God* (David C. Cook, 2009).

- Peter Scazzero, *The Emotionally Healthy Church* (Zondervan, 2003).

- Charlotte Allen, *The Human Christ: Search for the Historical Jesus* (Free Press, 1998).

- Robert W. Funk, *The Five Gospels: What Did Jesus Really Say? The Search for the Authentic Words of Jesus* (Macmillan, 1993).

- Marcus J. Borg, *Reading the Bible Again for the First Time: Taking the Bible Seriously but Not Literally* (HarperSanFrancisco, 2001).

Suggested Questions for Further Discussion/Thought

1. Does it compromise Jesus' ministry in any way if he ever was wrong? How?

2. There are accounts throughout the Old Testament of God changing his mind; does this imply that God can be wrong?

3. If we believe Jesus may have been wrong on occasion, how might this challenge our confidence in his vision for his own ministry?

Jesus forgave people of their sins before he died. How could he do this if he actually had to die in order to save us from sin?

···············
Phil Snider

For many years, I sat in church quietly wondering why God's forgiveness was based on the idea that awful violence had to be inflicted upon Jesus in order for God to save us from sin. I was never comfortable with this idea, but I feared voicing my questions would make my Christian friends think I was a hell-bound heretic.

It was only when I went to seminary that I learned this wasn't the only way to view Jesus' death, and I'm glad to say I no longer believe Jesus had to die in order to save us from sin.

As it turns out, the idea that Jesus had to die on the cross in order for God to forgive our sins took nearly a thousand years to develop, and numerous theologians have pointed to its problematic implications. Chief among these concerns are questions related to God's power and God's character. In terms of God's power, why is it necessary for God to sacrifice God's Son in order to grant forgiveness? Is there, as Frederiek Depoortere says, "some higher authority or necessity above God with whom God has to comply in doing this"?[22]

In terms of God's character, can't such a belief make God out to be "a *perverse* subject who plays obscene games with humanity and His own Son,"[23] like the narcissistic governess from Patricia Highsmith's *Heroine* who sets the family house on fire in order to be able to prove her devotion to the family by bravely saving the children from the raging flames?

Instead, my Christian faith is grounded in the affirmation that God's love is unconditional, which leads me to believe that God's forgiveness is unconditional as well. All of which means that Jesus' unconditional forgiveness—offered before he died—is one of the things that makes him most Godlike!

··························
Amy Reeder Worley

I'm a lawyer. My first reaction on reading this particular banned question was to leap from my desk and shout, "Objection! This question assumes facts not in evidence." Yes, I know that is weird. But it's also true. The question as posed assumes that Jesus had to die to "save" people from sin. I don't find much biblical or historical evidence to support this "substitutionary atonement" theory of Jesus' crucifixion and resurrection.

Rather I agree with Marcus Borg and other postmodern theologians who argue that Jesus died *because of* human sin, not in the place of humans who sin. As it relates to the question at hand, my view of the crucifixion means necessarily that forgiveness of sin emanates directly from God, and it existed before, during, and after Jesus' life and resurrection. Like many religious ideas, God's forgiveness operates outside of our limited view of space-time.

So how is it, exactly, that Jesus had the authority to forgive people? Sacred texts throughout the world speak of forgiving our enemies as a sacred and holy act. When Jesus forgave the unclean, criminal, and Gentile he embodied God's preexisting forgiveness of us all, teaching his followers that forgiveness was not limited to the religiously "in" crowd of the day.

In Matthew 9:1–8, Jesus forgives and then heals a paralyzed man. The rabbis accuse Jesus of blasphemy for claiming the authority to forgive sins, an authority they believed was reserved for YHWH. Jesus responds, "Why do you think evil in your hearts? For which is easier, to say, "Your sins are forgiven," or to say, "Stand up and walk"? But so that you may know that the Son of man has authority on earth to forgive sins, Jesus turned to the paralytic and healed him. The crowd was "filled with awe, *and they glorified God, who had given such authority to human beings."* Here, as throughout the gospels, Jesus reaffirms the message that God's love and forgiveness are available to all of us, all of the time.

....

Tripp Fuller

One could answer the question by saying that Jesus knew he was going to die and rise so he could forgive with the future known and certain or possibly that Jesus' divine identity gave him the ability to forgive sin at will, or one could even suggest that if forgiveness could be given before the cross, then the cross may not have been necessary.

In forgiving sins, Jesus is acting on behalf of God and was one of the reasons Jesus was opposed by the religious leaders, thus forcing one to explain how Jesus' identity is tied to that of God. To understand this, I have found it helpful to see how Paul reimagined the sacrificial system in light of Christ's work.

Traditionally an act of sacrifice began with the sinner transferring their identity to the animal through an act of consecration. Afterward the animal was killed so that the person was reincorporated into the people of God. Paul reverses the process so that it begins with Christ identifying with us and ends with the consecration, us identifying with that which is sacrificed.

In a sense Paul sees, in Christ, God coming to put an end to sacrifice by turning it upside down and beginning with God's coming to sinner with good news. From this perspective it would make sense that Jesus could forgive sin without having died because God had come in Christ to consecrate the world as God's beloved.

• • • • • •

Scriptural References

Matthew 9:2; 18:21; Mark 2:5; Luke 5:20; 7:48; 15:11–32; 23:34

Suggested Additional Sources for Reading

- Any of Marcus Borg's books on Jesus and Christianity
- Rita Nakashima Brock and Rebecca Ann Parker, *Proverbs of Ashes* (Beacon Press, 2002).
- Frederiek Depoortere, *Christ in Postmodern Philosophy* (T & T Clark, 2008).
- Slavoj Žižek, *The Fragile Absolute* (Verso, 2000) and *Did Somebody Say Totalitarianism?* (Verso, 2001).

Suggested Questions for Further Discussion/Thought

1. Do you believe that we have the authority to forgive each other in a religiously relevant sense?
2. Why do you believe Jesus was crucified? How does Jesus' forgiveness of sin before his death affect that belief?
3. Looking at the Bible verses mentioned previously, what types of people do the gospel writers talk about forgiving? Why do you think that is?
4. What import do you give to Jesus' statements of forgiveness from the cross?
5. Do you believe the blood sacrifice of an innocent person is necessary in order for God to forgive sin? Have you ever felt uncomfortable accepting this doctrine? If so, why?

Jesus broke certain biblical laws by healing on the Sabbath, associating with non-Jews, and not keeping all of the kosher laws. So how do we know which rules to follow and which are irrelevant to us today?

....

R. M. Keelan Downton

A The clearest place Jesus addresses the idea of rules is his sermon recorded in Matthew and Luke. His treatment of Torah "law" (I think "instruction" is generally a better translation) is essentially a critique of legalism, but not one that lets us off the hook.

Jesus both frees his listeners from a static prison of rules that are detached from real life situations and also invites them to explore their own intentions more deeply as a way to embody the reign of God. Jesus is not providing a new set of rules (that are more or less difficult to follow depending on how you look at them) but rather advocating a new way of thinking about the rules that focuses on the trajectories they create for communities and the way they support or inhibit relationships between humans and with all creation.

It is important to realize that, though Jesus gets into some arguments over this, he is not the first (or the last) Jewish teacher to approach the Torah this way. Figuring out which instructions given to ancient Hebrews can continue to lead us into wise living today therefore requires being in dialogue with a community about where obedience to such instruction would take the community. It is always a complex process and is made more so by the fact that so many people are part of multiple communities with differing norms.

Following Jesus in this endeavor means starting with the instruction to love God fully and following it with the instruction to love our neighbors with the same love we have for ourselves.

....

Amy Reeder Worley

A The Bible is internally inconsistent, so, as Karen Armstrong points out in *The Case for God*, "our reading is always selective." In fact, it is political. Throughout biblical history, religious teachers like Jesus have interpreted biblical texts through the lens of the political and cultural context of their time.

Jesus was a Jew living in Judea during Roman imperial rule. His world was one of wide-scale oppression, poverty, and disenfranchisement of religious and cultural minorities. His selective reading of Jewish texts offered an interpretation of Jewish law that spoke to the present political and cultural situation in Rome as he experienced it.

Jesus emphasized the "spirit" of Jewish law—liberation from spiritual and political oppression. In healing on the Sabbath, associating with non-Jews, and not keeping kosher, Jesus demonstrated a loving and compassionate Judaism that was less concerned with the edicts of the priesthood and more concerned with the suffering of people. His example teaches that religious legalism should not be used to oppress, exclude, or ignore God's people.

Consistent with Jesus' example, we should be cautious that we don't employ biblical literalism to injure God's people. Unfortunately Christianity, like most other monotheistic religions, has been used to justify slavery and poverty and as an alleged "reason" for natural disasters, disease, and pestilence. If anything, Jesus' message was that such actions are contrary to true faith.

. . . .

Chris Haw

The early church, we are told, saw a great many conversions. But what is most likely is that these early adherents were "God fearers," meaning they were Gentiles that had, previous to Jesus, associated themselves with the Jewish community by enjoying some of their festivals and customs. They already knew Jewish history. The common code of conduct that such persons had to obey was *not* the Mosaic law but only the Noachide covenant: refraining from meat sacrificed to idols, sexual immorality, and so on. The early church apparently used the same criteria, as seen in the book of Acts and Paul's teachings.[24]

But it is particularly provocative to note that the temptation of the early church was not to lean away from Judaism *but to become almost identical to it*. Many in the church thought that potential members should *join the entire story*, not only becoming God fearers, but fully initiated Jews through the Abrahamic ritual of circumcision and concomitant expectation of following all Mosaic laws. But the church rejected that approach and, almost sadly in my opinion, so little is expected of the average Gentile joiner—well, all except "believing in Jesus," which is no easy task.

Later, when Christianity spread into places that had not even heard about Jewish history, the church needed to train people in those stories— otherwise a "conversion" would be too fast, dry, and meaningless, seeing as

Jesus can only be seen when backlit by the Passover, exodus, the Prophets, the Temple and king stories, and so on. Once the church needed to labor at explaining these things it began the *catechumenate*, or entry process, of slowly bringing believers into the fold over a (sometimes three-year) long period of time.

In sum, Gentiles enter into the story of God's salvation "through faith" in Jesus—and what that means is quite a blur to me—and are only constrained to follow the Noahide law: refraining from blasphemy, idolatry, adultery, bloodshed, robbery, and eating flesh cut from living animals.[25]

····························
L. Shannon Moore

A. While Jesus did come to bring the good news, heal the sick, and reveal God in a new way, we have to remember that he did not want to throw the proverbial baby out with the bathwater. He grew up with the laws of his ancestors and, for the most part, seemed to keep them. He even said, "Do not think I have come to abolish the law or the prophets" (Matthew 5:17). Clearly, he thought the law was important. So why did he break some of them?

Well, let's take a look at one of the times when he did. In Matthew, Mark, and Luke, religious leaders criticize Jesus' disciples for plucking heads of grain to eat on the Sabbath. Jesus, defending them, references a story about the much-revered Israelite king David who also broke a law when he and his companions were hungry. In Mark's version he then says, "The [S]abbath was made for humankind, and not humankind for the [S]abbath" (Mark 2:27).

And I think that pretty much sums it up for us. Laws and rules are generally set forth for us to guide us, to protect us, and to lead us in certain directions. The biblical laws protected God's people from eating foods that might make them sick and gave them guidelines for moral behavior. But when we follow laws and rules to the extreme, they can become harmful (see the "Flagellants," the medieval sect who beat themselves and each other as a form of repentance).[26] We should follow the rules until they become destructive, harmful, or irrelevant.

····················
Peter J. Walker

A. In Mark 2, Jesus responds to questions about picking grain on the Sabbath: "The sabbath was made for humankind, and not humankind for the sabbath" (Mark 2:27). Clearly, Jesus was able to prioritize what was truly important. Can we be trusted to do the same? Whether we can or not, we're already doing it.

Countless books have been written to defend or discount every rule found in scripture; often the most devout people have the hardest time accepting "gray areas." But the God of scripture is a God of gray, and no example proves that point better than Jesus himself.

When Christians were persecuted in Acts 5, a revered Pharisee named Gamaliel cautioned the Sanhedrin, "So in the present case, I tell you, keep away from these men and let them alone; because if this plan or this undertaking is of human origin, it will fail; but if it is of God, you will not be able to overthrow them—in that case you may even be found fighting against God" (Acts 5:38–39).

As the church, we need to make room for God's voice among dissenters, rebels, and radicals. As individual believers, I advocate John Wesley's approach: urging Christians to weigh the voice of God through scripture, tradition, experience, and reason. None of these (not even scripture) is objectively reliable enough to trust alone. And we must honestly search our own motives: *Am I trying to prove a point, feed my ego, satisfy a hidden agenda, or stir division?*

In Matthew 12, Jesus says, "But if you had known what this means, 'I desire mercy and not sacrifice,' you would not have condemned the guiltless" (Matthew 12:7). Choosing how to interpret Biblical laws should never be a matter of condemnation or self-differentiation but of humble striving for wholeness, truth, and wisdom.

• • • • • •

Scriptural References

Matthew 5:17–18; 12:1–8; Mark 2:23–28; Luke 6:1–5; Acts 5:17–39

Suggested Additional Sources for Reading

- Karen Armstrong, *The Case for God* (Knopf, 2009).

- Marcus Borg, *Jesus: Uncovering the Life, Teachings, and Relevance of a Religious Revolutionary* (HarperSanFrancisco, 2006).

- Brian D. McLaren, *The Secret Message of Jesus: Uncovering the Truth That Could Change Everything* (Thomas Nelson, 2007).

- A. J. Jacobs, *The Year of Living Biblically: One Man's Humble Quest to Follow the Bible as Literally as Possible* (Simon and Schuster, 2008).

- William S. Campbell, *Paul and the Creation of Christian Identity* (T & T Clark, 2006).

- John Howard Yoder, *The Jewish-Christian Schism Revisited* (Eerdmans, 2003).

Suggested Questions for Further Discussion/Thought

1. What are some other examples of laws or rules that become dangerous when taken to extremes?

2. Does it demonstrate a lack of faith to question biblical laws rather than just following them because we are instructed to?

3. Where is the line between keeping the spirit of Jesus' teaching and theological relativism?

4. Do you think the Bible is a living document, subject to continuous interpretation, or a book that's "plain meaning" should be followed as literally as possible?

5. Did Jesus actually break the law, or was he privy to special insights we can't understand?

6. Jesus said in Matthew 7:12, "In everything do to others as you would have them do to you; for this is the law and the prophets." Can we take him at his word, or was he just trying to make a point?

7. Paul wrote in Galatians 5:14, "For the whole law is summed up in a single commandment, 'You shall love your neighbour as yourself.'" Can it be that simple? What happens if we live that way?

Can you be LGBTQ and be a Christian?
A minister? More denominations and
Christian communities are welcoming
LGBTQ people, as well as ordaining
LGBTQ as ministers. Is this really possible?

....
Andrew Marin

The answers to these questions are best described by a good friend of mine who is gay. He says, "If 'Christian' means I trust Jesus alone to bring me into right relationship with God, and if 'gay' means I experience sexual attraction and romantic feelings toward people of the same sex, then I qualify as a gay Christian. At one point I chose to be a Christian, and over a period of time, I discovered I'm gay.".

Contemporary society must start deconstructing its understanding of a gay Christian. Depending on who you ask, gay Christians are either fully acculturated LGBTQ people who have integrated their faith and sexuality, or they are oxymorons that can't actually exist. The expectation is that the correct response must land in only one of those two camps. The remaining question begs, then, what about the LGBTQ person who legitimizes his or her LGBTQ orientation and then chooses to be celibate based on a conservative theological interpretation? Can that person correctly self-identify as a gay Christian?

Many fighting this debate would suggest "no." And, denominationally, if one disagrees with "the other" regarding the various progressive and conservative interpretations of gay relationships and ordination, does that give the right to go ahead and justifiably delegitimize the realness of the other's conviction and filtration? There must be more nuance added to this conversation, even in what seems to be the most simple of questions.

....
Brian Ammons

When I was ordained I'd quite visibly identified with the local LGBTQ community for years. It was understood by the community where I was serving that my experiences as someone who had stood on the other side of religious-based violence was part of the gift I brought with me to my ministry. As a Baptist, our tradition is that the ordaining body is the congregation, so the decision was made at a local level. I was fortunate to be ordained and serve a community who knew me well and partnered with me in discerning a call to vocational ministry.

Our contemporary Western understandings of sexual identity are pretty different from the time and place in which Jesus lived. I think most of the church's current debate about LGBTQ inclusion is really about our diversity of views concerning sexual identity and scriptural hermeneutics. For example, if you think about sexual identity as being mostly made up of habits or behaviors, and you look to literal interpretations of the *King James Bible*, of course you'll see the ordination of LGBTQ folks as contrary to Christian teaching. However, if you understand sexual identity as a sacred gift drawing us into being more fully human through our desire to love and be loved, and you understand Scripture as a record of a people's experience of God in a specific time and place, which still has distinct and powerful meaning for us, it's totally reasonable that you would come to a different understanding.

While I might say that most of the positions we hear articulated can stand within the broader Christian tradition, it's not to say that they are all equally appropriate. In the end, the question for me is, Which is the more Christlike stance? —and I come down on the celebration of the gift of love.

....

Margot Starbuck

At the heart of this question, I hear the wondering, "Can someone that the Church has historically identified as a sinner be a Christian?" The asker could be a curious LGBTQ pagan or a wondering straight Christian or a doubting LGBTQ person raised in the Church. Regardless of the faith convictions or political opinions or moral leanings of the asker, whether affirming or judgmental, the "Christian" answer is *necessarily* a resounding yes. To suggest otherwise is just nutty.

Whether queer brothers and sisters are welcome by denominational bodies to shepherd flocks as pastors is another can of worms. Faithful and intelligent academics and pastors and laypeople within the network of congregations in which I am situated, the Presbyterian Church USA, have been debating this one for years. And years. And years. Those who welcome LGBTQ folks into leadership maintain, from Scripture, that committed monogamous relationships are not condemned in the biblical texts. Those who would deny ordination to LGBTQ folks maintain, from Scripture, that sexual intimacy is only permitted within the bounds of heterosexual marriage. Among this latter group, some do ordain LGBTQ Christian leaders who have chosen celibacy.

Though the Church continues to have a difficult time navigating this one, intelligent loving faithful folks do, in fact, host each of these opinions.

And while, in the midst of our differences, it's tempting to abandon relationship with the other, our calling is to practice genuine good-seeking love for one another. That is where the rubber hits the road.

·····································
Two Friars and a Fool

A. Not only is this possible, it's awesome! Lots of amazing people are now doing ministry openly that they've done throughout Christian history while being forced to hide who they really are. LGBTQ equality is the right side of history and is a movement of the Spirit in our age.

If you dig deep into the Bible, you can contort a half-dozen passages and claim they are referring to modern, committed, same-sex couples living out their sexual orientation as we now understand it. You're wrong, but you can make the case, and even make it sound kind of compelling. But why would you want to? Nothing in Scripture demands that we treat LGBTQ folks like less than people, less than fully made in the image of God, or any more sexually sinful than their straight neighbors. Outside of these half-dozen poor, contorted Bible passages, there is no justification whatsoever for this kind of behavior— not in ethics, nor in law, nor in the social or physical sciences. Not to mention the overwhelming witness of Scripture, which is that God is in the boundary-breaking business when it comes to love and the blessed community.

Right now, thousands of LGBTQ folks are ordained clergy, in multiple denominations, and are leading the body of Christ in worship, prayer, sacraments, and service. Many more LGBTQ people of faith are loving God and following Jesus and empowered by the Holy Spirit. Right now. You can't stop them, and why would you want to?

· · · · · ·

Scriptural reference(s):

John 13:34–35

Suggested additional sources:

- *Bulletproof Faith* by Candace Chellew-Hodge (progressive) *Out of a Far Country* by Christopher Yuan (conservative)

- A Loose Garment of Identifications by Brian Ammons (2010) http://homebrewedchristianity.com/2011/03/02/thats-too-gay-brian-ammons-banned-chapter-from-baptimergent/

- www.gaychristian.net – Gay Christian Network has a really useful booklet that helps congregations study the Scriptures on both "sides" of this issue. (I understand how even visiting the site could be a little anxiety-producing for some, but it really is a very fair, thoughtful, valuable resource. What makes GCN a particularly valuable resource to a variety of congregations is that it includes both affirming gay Christians and those who choose to practice celibacy.)

- *On Being Liked* by James Alison
- *Sex and the Single Savior* by Dale Martin
- *Jesus, the Bible, and Homosexuality: Explode the Myths, Heal the Church* by Jack Rogers
- http://twofriarsandafool.com/2010/10/lgbtq-ordination-resource
- http://twofriarsandafool.com/2009/03/not-a-sin-introduction/

Questions for further discussion/thought:

1. What is your understanding of a gay Christian?
2. Have a conversation with a theologically conservative gay Christian and a progressive gay Christian. Listen to their stories and notice the differences about how they came to formulate their understandings of labeling themselves as gay Christians.
3. How would our conversations about sexuality change if we were to focus less on questions of sexual identity and more on questions of sexual practice?
4. What would it look like to approach sex as a form of prayer?
5. What word could you put in this sentence to which the answer would be no? "Can you be _____ and be a Christian? (A discussion starter!)
6. To be a member of the Levitical priesthood, your body had to be whole and without defect, you had to be a male descendant of the right families, and you had to fulfill a wide variety of ritual purity requirements. When Jesus died, the curtain of the Holy of Holies was torn in half, signifying the end of the Levitical priesthood and universal access to God. Whom would Jesus exclude from the priesthood today, and why?
7. Have you ever met any people, or heard of any, who chose their sexual orientation?
8. Can you think of any way that a Christian leader's sexual orientation would make a difference in how he or she prays, worships, shares in the sacraments, counsels and serves people, etc.?

Source cited:

- *Love Is an Orientation: Elevating the Conversation with the Gay Community* by Andrew Marin (Downers Grove, Ill.: InterVarsity Press, 2009)

Preachers such as Joel Osteen preach about Jesus wanting us to be rich. Where does this belief come from? Wasn't Jesus poor? Didn't he tell rich people to give everything away?

....

Jonathan Brooks

The idea that Jesus wanted us to be rich is a very popular notion. As a representative of a group of people who have been marginalized and underresourced in this country for over a century, I understand why many minorities flock to this kind of teaching. Our white counterparts seem to enjoy the teaching because it does not challenge the American idea of comfortable living, even if it is at the expense of others. I simply remind people when they ask me this question that Jesus was obviously not a fan of the rich. He didn't hate them, but he always challenged them. When the rich young ruler came to Jesus to inquire about going to heaven, Jesus let him know that his main problem was his love for things. He told him to sell everything and then come back and follow him to see if he would really do it. Sadly, that was too much to ask of him. The truth is, our mistreatment of people and selfishness has lead to the prominence of this teaching. Being rich is not a bad thing, but it can be a problem. So much so that Jesus is quoted as saying it is easier for a camel to go through the eye of a needle than for a rich person to get into heaven. OUCH!

....

Margot Starbuck

Though God did promise prosperity the Israelites as they entered the promised land, the wacky Christian extraction of this—a la Osteen—is called the "health and wealth gospel." And though health and wealth are certainly values our *culture* endorses, they're nowhere to be extolled in the life or teaching of Jesus. Rather, repeatedly, in a variety of phrasings, Jesus exhorts his followers to lose their lives, to give them away, to sacrifice themselves, to bear their crosses, which is kind of the polar opposite of health and wealth.

Given our natural human predilection toward comfort, though, it's easy enough to convince ourselves that Jesus *does* want us to be happy, healthy, and rich by our clever reading of the Bible. When Jesus says, "Do not store up for yourselves treasures on earth" (Mt. 6:19a, NIV), we *hear*, "As long

as I don't have as much money as Brad Pitt and Angelina Jolie, I'm good."
When Jesus says "For where your treasure is, there your heart will be also"
(Mt. 6:21, NIV), we hear, "Even though my heart and mind perseverate on
making more money, and buying new shoes, and eating fudge sundaes, I
am totally *not* like Disney's greedy Scrooge McDuck, who runs gold coins
through his four-fingered duck-hands all day long…because I don't *own*
gold coins…. So, I'm probably good." And when Jesus says, "You cannot
serve both God and money" (Mt. 6:24, NIV), we hear, "I *can* serve God and
money" because we've been shaped more by our culture than by Christ.

················

Phil Jackson

I grew up poor, and when you grow up fighting over chicken wings,
you dream of a time when you can have enough money to buy
chicken wings for the whole block. No one likes being poor in a world that
advertises that you are not good enough unless you have *this* type of shoe,
this type of car, or *this* type of house. The poor often feel left out; therefore,
capitalism drives desire. When you live without, your life is defined more by
what you don't have than what you do have, even though in all reality you
are very wealthy in terms of community, family, and even in faith. It is not
glamorous to be poor; no one is filling out applications to be poor; you feel
less than human.

I believe this is the reason Christ came to preach the gospel to the
poor and to set the captives free. He taught in many stories how he came to
demonstrate the love of God to the "least of these." Jesus, in part, quoted
a passage of scripture from the Old Testament that defends the weak, the
stranger, and the oppressed, and teaches that this is as much an expression
of God's essence as creating the Universe. Christ was poor, very poor, as in
the "hood projects" poor, and spoke about money often—some say more
than he did about salvation. Christ knew that your heart will be where your
treasure is; therefore, if your heart is about influence, power, and money, then
everything tends to be seen from that vantage point.

The American Church has lost its identity and has substituted a
capitalistic agenda for Christ's agenda, all in the name of God. That is why
God is not in a lot of our churches, because of this substitution. You hear tons
of messages that center on provoking God to give to you as much as you
give to him, and thus you will prosper and have individual material success.
This avoids the central message of Jesus Christ to the poor. The American
Church has sought to follow America as its God rather than the one true
God, and its purpose is lost. You see the church grasping for gimmicks to
keep folks coming to church, and using the capitalistic language and agenda
of America. You even hear people saying, "We are church shopping." What
happened to serving, dying to self, and doing life with others to build the
kingdom of God?

According to the United Nations Human Development Report (2003), the richest 5 percent of the world's people receive 114 times as much income as the poorest 5 percent. In other words, twenty-five million Americans (the richest twenty-five million) enjoy as much income as the poorest two billion people in the world combined! Those who follow Christ should follow what he is passionate about, not what is popular or comfortable. Christians are to serve the poor, to love the least of these, to journey with each other in a community of faith, and live in wonder at how God meets our needs as we depend upon him and live interdependent with each other.

• • • • • •

Scriptural reference(s):

Deuteronomy 8:1–16; Psalm 146; Matthew 6:19–24; Matthew 19:24; Matthew 25:31–46; Mark 10:24; Luke 4:16–21; Luke 18:25

Suggested additional sources:

- *Following Jesus through the Eye of the Needle* by Kent Annan
- *Counterfeit Gods* by Timothy Keller
- *Rich Christians in an Age of Hunger: Moving from Affluence to Generosity* by Ronald Sider

Questions for further discussion/thought:

1. How does Jesus' quote about rich people and the eye of the needle affect your goals in life?
2. Would you still desire to be rich even if it meant that others in the world must remain poor?
3. In what ways do you see Christians divesting themselves of power and privilege in order to be more like Christ?
4. Can those with wealth truly partner to serve alongside the least of these? How?
5. What does an authentic Acts 2 community look like today?

Sources cited:

- *The Holy Bible*
- *Rich Christians in an Age of Hunger: Moving from Affluence to Generosity* by Ronald Sider (Dallas: Word Publishing, 1997)
- *United Nations Human Development Report 2003*, available at http://hdr.undp.org/en/reports/global/hdr2003/

Are Mormons, Jehovah's Witnesses, Seventh Day Adventists, Spiritists, Christian Scientists, etc., really Christians? Who gets to decide?

....

Doug Pagitt

A. The question of who gives approval for someone claiming to be a follower of Jesus has unfortunately been part of the faith from its founding. Jesus' disciples were accused of not being part of the faith of Abraham since they prayed wrongly. They, in turn, thought that those who were not doing faith their way were out, only to be corrected by Jesus that "whoever isn't against us is for us."

Christianity is not a faith in which there are certain cultural or belief quotas that must be met; rather, it is an opt-in faith. A people are part of the Christian tradition when they declare themselves to be.

Not only was it that way at the time of Jesus, it was so in the years afterward.

Christian is a cultural term assigned first to people in Antioch in the first century, and it is described in the book of the Bible called Acts in Chapter 11 verse 26. We are given a little nugget of understanding for how the term Christian was first used. It was given to non-Jewish followers of Jesus in Antioch who were following the teachings of Paul. But the Jewish believers did not consider these "Christians" to be a true part of the faith, so the term was used first to exclude them from the faith. Only later did it become the term used almost universally.

With the development over the last two thousand years of many versions of Christianity in varied cultures with opt-in faith beliefs, there is no standard-bearing group that gets to speak on behalf of all Christian traditions. Christianity is a faith in which all professions are included. In the words of Peter from the first century, we are all invited to see that "I really am learning that God doesn't show partiality to one group of people over another" (Acts 10:34, CEB).

....

Jonathan Brooks

A. This is a very touchy topic, because I personally would not place all of these groups into the same category. There are some basic things that you must hold to in order to be a Christian as defined by Jesus Christ himself. Some would say if they don't agree with repentance, acceptance of Christ's sacrifice, and unconditional love, Christ would tell us to wipe the dust off our feet and keep moving.

Personally, my issue with certain religious groups is really not their theology as much as their thoughts about people. Any religion that looks at one group as inferior to another, in my consideration, is not Christianity. Jehovah's Witnesses and Mormons have traditionally looked upon minorities as inferior to whites and are distinctly American religions. Prior to 1978, Mormons forbid blacks from joining the Mormon Church. I personally don't know who gets to decide whether they are Christians or not, but if you ask them, they will say emphatically that they are.

Seventh Day Adventists seem to follow the same guidelines as most Christians but add a Saturday Sabbath and dietary restrictions. I think additional preferences and denial of human rights are two very different issues, so I would not place them in the same category.

Each group must stand alone, and you as an individual must decide which groups are Christian according to your standards. I urge you to do your homework, and I think you will find we all have just as much in common as we have differences.

• • • • • •

Scriptural reference(s):

Matthew 7:22; Matthew 24:4–5; Acts 10:34; Galatians 1:8; Galatians 3:28

Suggested additional sources:

- *So What's the Difference?* by Fritz Ridenour
- *Kingdom of the Cults* by Dr. Walter Martin
- *Know What You Believe* by Paul E. Little

Do Christians have to be baptized? Why do some sprinkle while others immerse? Which one is "right"?

Brian Ammons

I'm a Baptist minister who was baptized (sprinkled) as an infant in the United Methodist Church. I've never been "re-baptized" through immersion, and though the tradition I claim as an adult follows an immersion practice, I value deeply my infant baptism. For me, to have been claimed as a child of God, beloved, sacred, and holy, before I had the language to even speak my name is a powerful and beautiful image. That blessing is mine, and no one can take it away from me. At times when I've felt some pretty vicious attacks coming from the church, that knowledge sustained me.

At the same time, I have stood chest deep in the baptismal waters with young adults resting back in my arms. I know the deep power and beauty of the "Believer's Baptism" ritual. Experiencing the profound abandon and deep trust that bodily submerging and emerging offers is tangible metaphor for a deeply profound inner experience. I feel immensely grateful to have been invited into that process with the people I lowered into and lifted out of those waters.

At this point in my journey, I am less tied to sacrament than I am to the sacramental. That is to say that I am less bound to the idea that there is a literal transformation in the baptismal process, the kind of thinking that gets really concerned about getting it right, but I am still invested in the idea that the ritual (whether sprinkled, poured, or immersed) is an outward and visible sign of an inward, transformational grace.

Margot Starbuck

Sprinkling is right. Whatever monkey business God does in baptism should definitely be moderated. Those hippy Jesus People in the seventies got dunked and went *way* overboard. In fact, even when sprinkling, have a towel nearby to wipe off any excess. Immediately.

Wait, did I say that out loud?

I meant: Dunking is right. Faith isn't just a top-of-the-*head* thing. It's something that you commit to with your whole being. If you're not dunked then you're probably holding back and not giving everything to Jesus. Dunking shows real commitment, because Jesus was dunked, not sprinkled.

I said that, too, didn't I?

The earliest Christian baptisms symbolized being plunged under dangerous waters into *death* with Christ. Dead—not *mostly* dead, but *dead-dead*—the believer is resurrected to new life with Christ. The old is gone and the believer's life is now a function of Christ's life within him or her. It's like the way Disney princesses, such as Snow White and Sleeping Beauty, slumber off into death and, once rescued, their lives then become a function of their rescuer-redeemer—for better or for worse.

Both sprinkling and dunking are physical signs of dying and rising to life with Christ. And though Christians too often make it about the christening gown or the catered after-party, it's really a fundamental sign of our Christian identity, meant to guide and form our Christlike living. Not to be a downer, but a life patterned after the cross of Christ is sort of…death-shaped—for better or for worse.

· · · · · ·

Scriptural reference(s):

Matthew 3:16

Suggested additional sources:

- *Grace for the Journey: Interpreting Baptist Ordinances for the 21st Century* by Cathy Tamsberg http://www.sitemason.com/files/fjcRTW/Grace%20for%20 the%20Journey.pdf

- *This Gift of Water: The Practice and Theology of Baptism among Methodists in America* by G. Felton

- http://en.wikipedia.org/wiki/Baptism

Questions for further discussion/thought:

1. What is the role of ritual in shaping our understanding of belonging to a community? What does it mean to belong?

2. Would you be able to give a persuasive argument for dunking? Sprinkling? Try to argue from the position you do not hold.

If all Christians basically believe the same thing, why do they have so many different denominations? And if there are so many denominations struggling to survive, why don't they just combine with other ones?

....

Hugh Hollowell

It is frustrating, isn't it? In a perfect world, we would all be one. In fact, Jesus prayed for that very thing. The reality is there are many different ways to engage a life of faith, and most denominations tend to focus on one over the others. and most people end up in the denomination that makes sense of how they engage God.

For example, Episcopalians tend to focus on liturgy or the ceremonies of the church, while Mennonites tend to focus on what happens during the week and in their community, and Presbyterians tend to be interested in scholarship. All three are legitimate ways of engaging God.

There are folks like myself who come to know things primarily through our bodies, so being Mennonite makes sense to me. Others are wired in such a way that they know things primarily by engaging their five senses, so the chanting and bells of the Episcopalians make more sense to them. Still others tend to live in their heads, so they want to know what the word was in the original Greek. These people are probably happy as Presbyterians. None of these are wrong—just different.

Most people are not that predictable in their church searching. It is just that we tend to end up at places that feel comfortable to us, and those places tend to have other people like us there.

....

Margot Starbuck

Throughout the centuries, various groups of Christians have, in essence, said, "In order to be in the club, you need to believe X, Y, Z." Sometimes, X, Y, and Z were issues core to the Christian faith. They were things such as, "Jesus' mom was a virgin," "Jesus is God's son," "Jesus rose from the dead," and "You don't get into heaven simply by paying money to the Church." They were clearly deal-breakers.

What's a deal-breaker for some folks, such as dunk baptisms or sprinkle baptisms, isn't a deal-breaker for others. Centuries of Church divisions have happened because some group of Christians truly believed in their hearts that whatever reason they were leaving over—a literal seven-day creation, women serving in church leadership, ordination of LGBTQ folks—really was, for them, a deal-breaker. So, while Christ's heart for his Church is unity, many Christians have had to follow their consciences and...split.

I think your suggestion for denominations to combine is just genius. While I suspect the answer for some in these smaller bodies who retain a clear memory of exactly what caused a local split and how very wrong the other side was is, "When hell freezes over," it's not unheard of. In the town where I live, I can point to two instances in the last five years of churches that split years ago being reunited under one holy roof. That, I am convinced, is a sign of the Kingdom.

• • • • • •

Scriptural reference(s):

John 17:18; 1 Corinthians 1:10

Questions for further discussion/thought:

1. If you had to trim down the "deal-breakers" to a bare minimum, what would they be?

2. What are the nonnegotiable essentials that you believe are central to the Christian faith?

Can someone be both an atheist and a Christian? If "Christian" actually means "follower of Christ," could someone be a student of the life of Jesus without accepting the claims of his divinity, or claims of the existence of any divinity at all?

. . . .

Jonathan Brooks

A. I suppose someone could follow Jesus in his humanity alone, although it is a bit of an oxymoron. It is very possible for people to be followers of Christ's moral teachings and still be atheists because they do not believe that Christ claimed to be God, and interpret those scriptures differently.

Jesus offers us so much more than mere wisdom. He offers us access to something and someone far greater. Jesus tells us in John that we must stay connected to him in order to produce the outcomes of his teachings, so trusting him as Lord is part of trusting him as teacher. My friend Brad would say it this way: *You are a toaster and God is the socket. Unless you stay plugged in to him, you will not toast anything.* Although having a toaster in our kitchen, admiring it, and reading the manual about all of the great toast it makes would be fine, it would still be weird to never plug it in to its power source and see it really do its job—toast things. To me, this is equivalent to following Jesus in his humanity and not believing in his deity. You can get great teachings and gain great knowledge, but the power behind those words comes from the Spirit of God. The Spirit of God is gained through accepting Jesus as Lord and Savior.

. . . .

Phil Snider

A. There are a lot of people who value Jesus' teachings but have a hard time accepting claims of his divinity. Depending on how you interpret Jesus' words in Mark 10:18 ("Why do you call me good?… No one is good— except God alone" [NIV]), even Jesus himself was hesitant to accept claims of his own divinity.

By the time the Gospel of John was written (several years after Mark was written), storytellers had become much more concerned with portraying Jesus as divine. When we hear verses such as John 14:6 ("I am the way and the truth and the life. No one comes to the Father except through me" [NIV]), it leads us to think that only those who believe in God ("the Father") can be a Christian. Yet according to Frederick Buechner, if we pay close attention, Jesus "didn't say that any particular ethic, doctrine, or religion was the way, the truth, and the life. He said that he was. He didn't say that it was by believing or doing anything in particular that you could 'come to the Father.' He said that it was only by him—by living, participating in, being caught up by, the way of life that he embodied, that was his way." All of which leads Buechner to conclude that it's "possible to be on Christ's way and with his mark upon you without ever having heard of Christ, and for that reason to be on your way to God though maybe you don't even believe in God."

···································
Two Friars and a Fool

Many people already self-identify as both atheist and Christian. Groups such as the Christian Humanists and Non-Theistic Christians are doing just that—following Jesus, practicing Christianity, but for the most part holding to a naturalistic worldview where there is no supernatural or transcendent God.

In fact, the earliest Christians were called atheists by their neighbors because they refused to worship anyone but Christ. There is an anti-superstition impulse deep in the heart of Christianity. As Peter Rollins likes to say, to believe is human; to doubt is divine.

It is true, though, that the Jesus we read about in the Gospels seems to have believed in a transcendent, supernatural God, and is described as performing acts we would now call miracles—such as restoring sight to the blind, walking on water, and so on. For some Christians, it is necessary for these things to be historically true. God must be in some way outside the world, and also able to act directly in the world.

For other Christians this is not as important. We don't call ourselves Non-Theistic Christians or Christian Humanists, but we don't have a problem calling people who do identify that way brothers and sisters in Christ. They can be more than just students of the life of Jesus—they can be "doers of the Word." They can live out the title "Christian," "little Christs," in their daily lives just as well as we can.

· · · · · ·

Scriptural reference(s):

Matthew 21:28–32; Mark 10:18; John 14:6

Suggested additional sources:

- www.atheists-for-jesus.com
- *The Human Being* by Walter Wink
- *Wishful Thinking* by Frederick Buechner
- www.christianhumanist.net
- http://www.nontheistfriends.org/

Questions for further discussion/thought:

1. Does it take credibility away from Christ's other teachings if you deny his claims of his own divinity?
2. Is Christianity primarily about belief or action? Why or why not? Is it possibly a combination of both? If so, why?
3. In the parable of the two sons, Jesus says that God is happier with the son who is wrong in word but right in deed than with the son who is right in word but wrong in deed. What do you think this may have to say about Christians and atheists?
4. Whether you think an atheist can be a Christian or not, what do you see as the minimum a person must believe, say, or do in order to be a Christian?

Sources cited:

- *The Holy Bible*
- *Wishful Thinking* by Frederick Buechner (New York: Harper & Row, 1973), p. 14
- *Insurrection* by Peter Rollins (Nashville: Howard Books, 2011)

What do Christians believe about disaster and suffering in the world? If God has a plan, why is suffering part of it? How do Christians reconcile suffering in their own lives?

······················

Andrew Marin

Unexpected deaths. Shattered dreams. Infertility. Betrayals. Unmet goals and prayers. Like anyone else I have had my share of suffering that can't be explained by any rational thought process. So how do I still have a faith in a God that I believe has a good plan? Because God never said, let alone promised, there would be no suffering. In fact, the Bible says just the opposite.

I believe people use suffering as an easy excuse to blame God, to point the finger at someone else, or to not have faith at all. Those are all too easy options of escapism. For me, suffering is an opportunity to actually live my faith when it matters the most. Anyone can live a good faith when things are great. Suffering doesn't make life or faith easy, right, justified, or satisfying. It makes it real.

In the midst of my pain and often-cried tears I can still call God's name and be thankful for an opportunity to live and feel and try to love through it all. In the midst of suffering is when I've been most real with God. I have nowhere else to turn; no one else to call upon. It's me and God. Together. Not in some cliché way that God will make it all better, but a hopeless-filled place where the rubber meets the road by practicing what I preach. In some twisted way it's where I feel connected to God the most.

······························

Matthew Paul Turner

The disciples asked Jesus a multiple choice question: Why was this man born blind? Was it (a) because he had sinned, or (b) because his parents had sinned? Jesus refuses both of their karmic options and proposes that the man's blindness presents an opportunity for God's glory to be shown. No, Mark Driscoll, I don't think he's indicating that God caused the man to go through a lifetime of blindness because one day Jesus was going to happen to walk by, and he would need someone to perform a miracle on to impress his friends. I think Jesus is reframing the entire scenario. What if Jesus is suggesting that suffering isn't an intellectual dilemma in need of a satisfying explanation? As anyone who has truly suffered knows, explanations of suffering aren't really that helpful. What if, instead, Jesus is suggesting that any instance of suffering presents an opportunity for those who would follow this God to partner with him in bringing healing into sickness, light into darkness, hope into despair.

The Bible doesn't attempt to offer a satisfying answer to the question of suffering. Instead, it describes a God who suffers with us and issues a call for us to embody a response rather than offer an explanation. We are not to insulate ourselves from suffering. We are to be the ones who enter into the suffering of others to help them bear it. As agents of hope, it is our calling to reflect and embody this God where he cannot be easily found.

. . . .

Hugh Hollowell

In my own faith, I have found it most helpful to think of it like this: God does have a plan to deal with the hungry children in Africa, a plan to ease the suffering of the sick, a plan to feed the hungry, a plan to comfort the afflicted.

God has a plan, and God's plan is us.

That children are hungry in a world where one in three of us are obese is not a failure of God, but a failure of us to live up to our part of God's plan. Often, Christians pray for God to act to ease suffering, when it is, in fact, God who waits on us to act.

● ● ● ● ● ●

Scriptural reference(s):

John 15:20; Romans 5:3–5; 1 Peter 4:12

Suggested additional sources:

- *A Theology of the Dark Side* by Nigel Goring Wright
- *Come Be My Light* by Mother Teresa
- *Evil and the Justice of God* by N. T. Wright
- *Friendship at the Margins* by Christopher Heuertz and Christine Pohl

Questions for further discussion/thought:

1. What is the first thing you do when you feel suffering?
2. Talk about the unanswered questions you still have about times of suffering in your life.

Source cited:

- *The Holy Bible*

It seems as if most Christians focus a lot more on issues of sex and sexuality than any other issue. Why?

....

Andrew Marin

The Church's pushback during the sexual revolution was to clearly instill the message that sex is a sacred gift of unity from God to be experienced with one's partner within a marriage context. This thought is the basis to why Christians are to wait to have sex until their wedding night. Though theologically correct, the Church has disproportionated this interpretation of love and sex as "the greatest gift God has given two people committed to each other for life." The problem, then, is that the past few generations of Christians have been proffered incorrect teachings and over-generalizations that have taken it one step further: sex is the greatest amount of love one can give to another.

The Bible says no such thing. What the Bible actually says is that the greatest expression of God's love to humanity is that God conforms us to the likeness of Christ. The Bible also says that the greatest expression of our love toward one another is to love God and love others like we have been first loved by God.

There is no hint of sex in any of those commands. Paul went so far to say that it is better to stay unmarried and serve God. However, if that is too difficult a task, it is then better to get married than to burn in hell with lust! In most scenarios the Church's overemphasis on sex is completely opposite to what the Bible actually teaches about love.

....

Brian Ammons

On the one hand, I'm not sure I agree with the premise of the question. I think Christians talk around sex and sexuality a lot, but rarely get to talking about it directly. In fact, I think many Christians put a lot of energy into trying to avoid serious conversations about sex and sexual practice. I'm longing for some serious conversation about sex, about what works, why it's beautiful and sacred, and how to approach it as a form of prayer. I want to hear Christians talk about those things, but most of what I'm hearing are debates about who can do what with whom, and, if they are doing *that*, if they can then teach Sunday school. We make a mockery out of the sacred gift of sex.

On the other hand, it seems as if we live in a sex-saturated culture. It's not just Christians focusing on sex—it's the nightly news; it's prime-time television; it's the self-help industry. Part of why I wish Christians were really talking about sex is because so many of us are so hungry for a counter-narrative to the commodification of bodies and intimacy that we experience in the world. What would a sex-positive, Christian perspective based in spiritual practice look like?

So, while I am invested in continuing and promoting a conversation about sex and sexuality among Christians, I want a different one than the one that seems to be drawing our attention. I want that conversation to take its place alongside other spiritual practices and to find enough room for us to sit with our differences in the same way we do around how we baptize, worship, and pray.

....

Phil Jackson

For Christians, the issue of sex is often associated with shame, whether it is shame from personal history, family, or the abuse they see happening in their community. As Christians, the Bible teaches that we are to refrain from sex before marriage and that sex is for the marriage bed; but marriages, even Christian marriages, are falling apart all over the place. In addition, especially where I live and serve on the west side of Chicago, we have more baby mommas than wives, the highest rate of HIV among men and high STDs among youth and women. There is an urgency to prevent or stop all this pain; therefore, this bemoaning of inappropriate sexual behavior becomes a bandwagon issue for a lot of people to talk about. Yet why don't Christians talk about the other issues, such as what the circumstances are that cause people to have sex before marriage, or what part abuse plays in some of the promiscuity. The reason is because that would take a longer commitment, and perhaps involve walking with someone who is struggling. It might even expose the systems that cause the problems (which Christians or others may be benefitting from), thus causing those Christians to lose whatever benefits that system may have given them. The issues are hard and many, yet shining the light of Christ upon some of the darkest issues we face is exactly what Christ has called us to do.

....

Phil Shepherd, a.k.a. The Whiskey Preacher

I have this game I play with Stephanie, my wife—and, no, it's not *that* kind of game either (insert sly grin here). This game is an amalgamation of "Slug Bug" and "I Spy." While we're driving, every time I spot a Cadillac, I yell "Cadillac!" This annoys the hell out of Stephanie and, in reality, I am the only one really playing the "Cadillac" game. You see, I have always wanted to own a Cadillac. My father always wanted one, too, but my mother wouldn't let him have one. And my wife Stephanie thinks they are ugly and useless. "Our Toyota rides just as nice as a Cadillac," she has told me on more than one occasion. That's heresy at its finest, folks.

The more Stephanie tells me no, the more I talk about procuring a Cadillac by any means necessary (within the law…of course). Sex and sexuality, for many Christians, are like a Cadillac for me. If something is seen as unattainable or taboo, then it's human nature to obsess about what you can't have. At some point in our Western puritanical past, this idea materialized: if it was pleasurable, it equaled sinful. Sex became something you can't have, can't talk about. We have a legacy of trying to annex off our sexuality from our humanity, squashing this beautiful part of how we were created. I can't have a Cadillac; that becomes all I want to talk about. For Christians who haven't been free to talk about sex, now that's all they want to talk about.

● ● ● ● ● ●

Scriptural reference(s):

Genesis 2:24–25; Matthew 22:36–40; Romans 8:28–30; 1 Corinthians 7:8–9; Hebrews 13:4

Suggested additional sources:

- *A Framework for Christian Sexual Ethics* by Margaret A Farley
- *Bringing Sex into Focus* by Caroline J. Simon (conservative)
- *God and Sex* by Michael Coogan
- *Real Sex* by Lauren F. Winner
- *Sex at Dawn* by Christopher Ryan and Cacilda Jetha (progressive)
- *Sexual Politics, Sexual Communities* by John D'Emilio (second edition)
- *The God of Sex* by Peter Jones
- *Sex and the Church* by Kathy Rudy
- *Body and Soul: Rethinking Sexuality as Justice-love* by M. Ellison and S. Thorson-Smith, eds.
- *The Ethics of Sex* by M.D. Jordan
- *A Loose Garment of Identifications* by Brian Ammons (2010), http://homebrewedchristianity.com/2011/03/02/thats-too-gay-brian-ammons-banned-chapter-from-baptimergent/
- *The Meaning of Sex* by Dennis Hollinger

- *Sex and Love in the Home* by David Matzo-McCarthy
- *The End of Sexual Identity* by Jennell Williams Paris

Questions for further discussion/thought:

1. What were you taught about sex growing up by your family and/or your church?
2. Does it differ from your understanding today, or what you will/might teach your own kids?
3. Do I see the gospel as holistic?
4. What are the issues I see that I don't get involved in and/or don't want to get involved in?
5. Have you compartmentalized your sexuality from your spirituality, and has that affected your overall life?

Source cited:

- *The Holy Bible*

I hear Christians say all the time that, good or bad, everything happens for a reason. What about genocide? Famine? Rape? What could the reason possibly be? Does there have to always be a reason?

. . . .

Brian Ammons

A. I don't buy it. I understand that it is comforting how some people believe that the world is orderly and reasonable in some plan we can't understand. I find exactly the opposite to be true. If the deep suffering of genocide and rape is a part of God's plan, God seems to be pretty sadistic. What makes more sense to me is to believe that God is with us in our suffering—that, when all else has crumbled, we are not alone. While I resist the idea that God puts suffering into our lives for a purpose, I do believe that when we hold our pain loosely enough to invite God into it with us, it can be transformed and become purposeful.

The most concrete example of this in my own life is my experience as a survivor of childhood sexual violence. I do not hold God accountable for the choices that my abuser made. I tried that… It just left me angry and dead inside. But, as I've done work toward my own healing, I've been able to experience the journey that has come out of that abuse as full of grace and life. It's led me to work with young people, commit my life to engaging the church in complicated conversations, and deeply connect with vulnerable people. That's where God is for me. Not in the reason behind the suffering, but in the transformation of the suffering into hope. God is in the practice of resurrection.

. . . .

Adam J. Copeland

A. Everything does happen for a reason, but let's not blame all the reasons on God. Just because an event is tragic does not mean God, with a conniving evil laugh, micromanaged the crisis from on high.

Take, for example, the fact that smoking cigarettes causes cancer. When a person who has smoked a pack a day for thirty years is diagnosed with cancer, there is "a reason" for the cancer. When a person with poor balance cleans the gutters, falls off a slippery roof, and breaks a leg, there is "a reason" for the broken bone. When a person drinks too much, then drives a car and causes a wreck, there is "a reason" for the incident.

The trick, in all these cases, is the right balance of noting the causes without blaming the person in need. We know that many cancers, household injuries, and car accidents are preventable, but that does not mean we should treat those affected with anything less than the utmost love and care.

Beyond these more clear reasons, however, I certainly admit that some events are so tragic, so dire, so horrifying that they defy all attempts at explanation. Indeed, in many cases even the most logical analysis of a tragedy's causes does not soothe one bit.

Ultimately, I cannot believe in a God who would engineer such tragedies as genocide, famine, and rape. I do believe, however, in a God who loves us through every trial and stays with us even to the deepest pit of despair.

Hugh Hollowell

A. Often, people who say things like that are people in pain who are searching for an explanation for things that otherwise make no sense, such as, to use your examples, rape or famine.

Sometimes bad things happen. In the Christian worldview, this is because we do not live in accordance with the plan God has for us. But regardless of why, sometimes bad things happen.

One helpful way to look at this is not that God causes these things to happen for a reason, but that God can use the bad things that do happen to accomplish good things such as the spirit of unity and love that came out of the tragedy of 9/11. God did not cause it, but God can use the bad things that happen to move God's dream for the world forward.

Margot Starbuck

A. It is human nature to prefer certainty over doubt or ambiguity. We'd rather be sure than unclear. We'd rather know than not know. Because uncertainty leaves room for anxiety to rise in our hearts, we'd much prefer to quell our fears, to soothe ourselves, with bold pronouncements of doctrinal certainty. "Everything happens for a reason" is one of those. I suspect it's this natural human temptation to relieve our own anxieties, rather than the revealed will or character of God, which causes us to make sweeping generalizations in an effort to explain what we don't understand.

Technically, of course, it is often true. One reason for genocide is the sinful segregation of peoples. A reason for famine is greed and inequitable distribution of resources. An explanation for rape is that a person who hurts deeply is someone who, himself, has been hurt deeply. Because there are twisted sinful reasons for human brokenness and depravity, however, does not make God the *author* of those reasons. In the release of God's people from captivity in Exodus, God is revealed as one who delivers threatened and oppressed people. In the wilderness, God provides for the hungry. In the person of Jesus, the bread of life, God feeds both souls and stomachs. In the Old Testament and again in the person of Jesus, God does not violate vulnerable women, but delivers and redeems them.

God is not a twisted dictator who inflicts suffering in order to teach people lessons. Though this interpretation may bring comfort or relief to some, it is a misrepresentation of the God who is revealed in the Scriptures as a redeemer and deliverer.

· · · · · ·

Scriptural reference(s):

Psalm 139; 1 Corinthians 14:33; Ecclesiastes 3:1–8; James 1:13; 1 John 1:5

Suggested additional sources:

- *Faith and Other Flat Tires: Searching for God on the Rough Road of Doubt* by Andrea Palpanat Dilly

- *Where Is God When Disaster Strikes?* (Adult Study) by Wendy Farley, The Thoughtful Christian, http://www.thethoughtfulchristian.com/Products/TC0067/where-is-god-when-disaster-strikes.aspx

- Read some Moltmann...any Moltmann

- Brian Ammons: http://homebrewedchristianity.com/2011/02/21/reframing-sexuality/

- http://www.ivpress.com/title/exc/1423-8e.php

Questions for further discussion/thought:

1. When have you felt these questions have been answered or not answered?

2. Does every situation need a reason?

3. What is the most troubling reality for you to reconcile with God's goodness and power?

4. Even if you believe that human suffering isn't authored by God, what sort of a letter of complaint might you like to address to the Almighty? (God can take it.)

Where does the idea that so many Christians and political leaders maintain about the United States being a Christian nation come from? Do all Christians believe this?

....

Carol Howard Merritt

A. "Can you see the Bible? Right there on that table," she pointed, without touching the precise oil brush strokes. "It's clear that our founders were God-fearing people."

My husband, Brian, and I squinted and nodded politely at the artist's rendering of a thick book. When the tour guide walked to the next work of art, I couldn't help but share a smile with Brian. It was our first time in our nation's capitol building and the third time we played "spot the Bible" in a painting.

We were guests of a family friend, a politician who rose to power during the Gingrich Revolution. Newt Gingrich armed the Religious Right for the Republican agenda. On this tour, every statue and painting had one point: it proved that the United States was a Christian nation. And the subtext followed: we Christians needed to take our nation back.

Yes, some people came to the United States with utopian visions of it being the "promised land." But we do not have a state-sanctioned church or a church-sanctioned state. We keep church and state separate. In recent decades, the Republican Party used "family value" issues, such as working against women's choice and same-sex rights, to keep conservative Christian Baby Boomers engaged, organized, and voting. The strategy will soon backfire, though, as younger Christians care more about starving people, ravaging wars, and environmental destruction than who's sleeping with whom.

Other Christians do not want the United States to become a theocracy. We want to make sure we maintain religious freedom for all Americans, whether they are Christians, Jews, Buddhists, Muslims, Hindu, Sikh, or none of the above.

....

Matthew Paul Turner

A. Not all Christians adhere to this understanding of American history. I don't, at least not anymore. But I do understand this type of thinking, since I was raised in a conservative Baptist church, one that adhered to the teaching that the United States was/is a "Christian nation." Some of the people at my church talked about the early settlers, the Pilgrims and Puritans who came to the New World for religious freedom, as if they were "New Israelites" or an updated version of "God's People" venturing into a God's new "promised land." John Winthrop once wrote that his hope was to make New England "as a city on a hill," a phrasing from the gospel of Matthew. Many Pilgrims/Puritans believed that their adventure was ordained by God to create a society that corrected all of the wrongs done by the Old World in the name of God.

This belief that the United States was/is a "Christian nation" is particularly important to America's brand of fundamentalism because it creates an easy-to-comprehend mental picture of a slope, one that they say showcases just how far the United States has slid down (and away) from the Puritanical ideals that this nation was "founded" upon, or the "Christian moral standards" it once valued. While it's true that many of our founding fathers viewed these ideas as an extension of their Christian faith, we also know that many others embraced these same ideas, not because of a great faith in God, but because they believed they were the good and right things to do.

....

Phil Jackson

Hell no, we are not a Christian nation! In the same way that statement is an oxymoron, it is an oxymoron to say our country is a Christian nation. Just using the language of Christianity without being submitted to its purpose is hypocritical. However, it all depends upon your perspective of what you mean by a Christian nation.

Do you mean by Christian nation one that is founded by a group of leaders who started our country and lived double lives, only bringing God in when it was convenient, but keeping him in his little department the rest of their lives? Only bring him in when they needed to justify their actions? Keeping slaves as a way of life but not seeing them as humans created in the image of God, somehow omitting the slaves they owned from the equation when writing the founding documents of this country? If this is what is meant by a Christian nation, then I guess you're justified in calling it that.

Our political leaders use what is popular at the time to get the votes of the people, but to truly call ourselves a Christian nation means a lot more than what has been practiced. In some way America sought to give off an image that, because of the faith of our leaders, we would all fall in line with their faith. Constantine the Great was a Roman emperor from 306 to 337. Well known for being the first Roman emperor to convert to Christianity, Constantine and co-emperor Licinius proclaimed religious tolerance of all religions throughout the empire. People gave lip service to the emperor in order to win approval and gain some mobility or acceptance, but only a few were true to the faith. This history, perhaps, is where we get the idea of the America assumption of being a Christian nation, yet it crushed all that were pure about the faith. If we were seeking to live out, as a nation, what Jesus taught—that blessed are those who are the peacemakers for they will be called sons of God, or blessed are the meek for they shall inherit the earth— we would look and live a lot different.

• • • • • •

Scriptural reference(s):

Matthew 5:1–12

Suggested additional sources:

- *Raised Right: How I Untangled My Faith from Politics* by Alisa Harris
- *Crazy for God: How I Grew Up as One of the Elect, Helped Found the Religious Right, and Lived to Take It All (or Almost All) of It Back* by Frank Schaeffer
- "Alisa Harris and Raised Right," *God Complex Radio* by Derrick Weston, http://godcomplexradio.com/2011/11/gcr-5-4-alisa-harris-and-raised-right/
- *The History of the Church: From Christ to Constantine* by Eusebius (author), Andrew Louth (ed., Introduction), G. A. Williamson (trans.)

Questions for further discussion/thought:

1. Does your faith inform your activism? Do politics inform your faith?
2. Do you think there is a problem with Christianity being so closely identified with the Religious Right?
3. What sort of problems do churches face when they allow a political party to set their agenda?
4. Do Christian principals cover all people equally?
5. Who should determine the interpretation of Christian principals if a nation sought to engage someone for that purpose?

Sources cited:

- *Utopia: The Search for the Ideal Society in the Western World* by The New York Public Library (Cambridge: Oxford University Press, 2001)
- *The History of the Church: From Christ to Constantine* by Eusebius (author), Andrew Louth (ed., Introduction), G. A. Williamson (trans.)
- "A Model of Christian Charity," a sermon by John Winthrop, 1630. available on many websites

How is it that so many Christians support, or even call for, wars when one of the names for the Christ they supposedly follow is "Prince of Peace," and Jesus urged love for enemies and nonviolent responses?

....

Carol Howard Merritt

The issue of war is complicated, both in our Scriptures and our tradition. The Old Testament is fraught with horrific stories in which God calls for the complete annihilation of men, women, and children. Jesus was called the Prince of Peace, but even Jesus said perplexing things such as, "Do not think that I have come to bring peace to the earth; I have not come to bring peace, but a sword" (Mt. 10:34, NRSV). Many followers expected Jesus to triumph over the oppressive Roman government, but Rome crucified him instead.

Our Christian tradition varies widely. While strong pacifist thought flows throughout Christianity, many Christians held tightly to the Just War Theories of Augustine of Hippo and Thomas Aquinas. They stated that war could be waged if there was a just cause, a properly instituted authority waged the war, and peace was the central motive in the midst of violence.

Of course, Augustine was writing during the fourth and fifth century when no one could imagine nuclear annihilation. No one could foresee that the United States would spend more on its military than the rest of the world combined. No one could dream of the barbarism that the richest country in the world could accomplish in strip bombing the poorest countries. No one could imagine how one nation could be so powerful that they could fight two wars without having hardly any impact on its citizenry. There is no way to compare the Old Testament annihilation of a fortified village or what Augustine described with the destruction we now accomplish with the press of a button.

American Christians need to struggle long and hard before they imagine any war that we pursue as just.

Christian Piatt

A. In his book, *Jesus and Nonviolence: A Third Way*, Walter Wink dismantles the myth that Jesus was a pacifist. Far from it, actually. Things like turning the other cheek and walking the second mile, in the context of Wink's nonviolent activist engagement, take on unexpected power, much like a black belt in aikido uses the energy of his attacker to overthrow him.

The great deception, says Wink, is that we Western-minded folks have bought the idea that we have two choices when faced with violence, injustice, or oppression: fight back in kind or do nothing. What is required, he says, is a third option, as modeled by Jesus, one that too often Christians and other people of faith mistake as a call for non-involvement.

As Wink claims, doing nothing in response to injustice is to implicitly support the violence already being done. But by acting in kind toward our enemy, we perpetuate the violence, becoming no better in many ways than the wrong to which we are responding.

Wink also effectively dispels the myth that violence, in any instance, has ever been a more effective tool than a nonviolent response. Ultimately more blood is shed and more people die, even if it's in our nature to want an eye for an eye.

Many of us can't think of the way Wink understands the teaching and life of Jesus as really a possibility for us. But, ultimately, it depends on how you measure success. If we consider the end of Jesus' ministry to be his moment of crucifixion—alone, vulnerable, and betrayed by those he continued to love—then his life's mission was a failure.

If, however, we believe that one life—perhaps even our own—is worth giving up for a change that brings hope to thousands or millions of others, many of whom we may never meet, then this third way begins to look like a path worth exploring and trying to imagine.

Two Friars and a Fool

A. God abhors violence. Human cruelty is the reason God repents of creation in the story of the flood. The law Israel receives from God on Mt. Sinai is replete with statutes designed to limit violence and urge mercy toward outsiders.

The prophets Isaiah and Jeremiah counseled total disarmament in the face of invasions by Assyria and Babylon, saying that their only security lay in God. Micah looked forward to the reign of God's Shalom as a time when the world would turn implements of war into tools of production, and no one would learn war anymore.

Jesus rejected multiple opportunities to be a militant messiah, commanded his disciples to put away their swords, and forgave his murderers while they were still in the act of executing him. When Jesus returned triumphant, he did not whisper a word of retribution against Rome, but offered further forgiveness to the disciples who had betrayed him and told them to take his peace into all the world. His earliest followers universally eschewed any form of violence, choosing martyrdom by the hundreds rather than pick up a sword in self-defense.

Paul, a violent zealot before Jesus found him, was one of those martyrs. He died proclaiming that we share Christ's ministry of reconciliation, that God is abolishing all divisions between people, and that our only enemies are spiritual ones.

We cannot carry both a cross and a sword. A person can either follow Christ or engage in violence, but not both at the same time.

· · · · · ·

Scriptural reference(s):

Genesis 6:9–13; Exodus 21:1–27; Leviticus 19:17–18; 24:19–22; Deuteronomy 19:1–7; Isaiah 11:1–10, 36–39, 65:17–25; Jeremiah 21; Micah 4; Matthew 4:1–11; 5:38-40; 10:34; 26:52; 28:19 ;Luke 4:1–13; 6:27–36; 22:36; 23:34; John 18:11; 20:19–23; 21:15–19; Acts 7:54–60; 9:1–19; 2 Corinthians 5:18–21; Galatians 3:28; Ephesians 6:12;Revelation 21

Suggested additional sources:

- *Jesus and Nonviolence: A Third Way* by Walter Wink
- http://gandhifoundation.org/resources/
- *The Autobiography of Martin Luther King, Jr.* by Martin Luther King Jr., Clayborne Carson, ed.
- *The Hunger Games Trilogy* by Suzanne Collins
- *War Is a Force That Gives Us Meaning* by Christopher Hedges
- *Readings in Christian Ethics: A Historical Sourcebook* by J. Philip Wogaman and Douglas M. Strong, eds.
- *The Politics of Jesus* by John Howard Yoder
- *The Powers that Be* by Walter Wink
- *The Power of Non-violence* by Martin Luther King Jr.

Questions for further discussion/thought:

1. Was Jesus a pacifist? Did he ever justify or demonstrate the use of violence?

2. How do you understand the Christian response to injustice, violence, or oppression?

3. Is there ever justification within the context of the Christian faith to respond to any situation with violence?

4. What are your personal memories of war?

5. What do you know about the many wars of the last thirty years? Can you name them all?

6. Do you hold to a Just War theory? Are you a pacifist? What do you think about war?

7. Jesus said, "Blessed are the peacemakers, for they shall be called children of God" (Mt. 5:9, NRSV). What does it mean to be a peacemaker in your context?

8. Whether you agree with the above or not, what do you think of people who identify as Christian but serve in the military or the police, where they carry weapons and may be called upon to kill someone? What do you think Jesus would say to people serving in the military or police forces in your country?

9. Is there a situation in which you could imagine yourself killing another human being? Why or why not?

Source cited:

- *Jesus and Nonviolence: A Third Way* by Walter Wink (Minneapolis: Fortress, 2003)

How do some Christians use their faith to oppose abortion, while also supporting the death penalty or personal gun rights?

Carol Howard Merritt

"You shall not kill" is a simple command that Christians recognize, but how it affects our beliefs and behaviors can be surprisingly complicated. There doesn't seem to be much logical consistency to the notion that life is so important that a fetus ought to be protected from the moment of conception, but anyone should have the right to bear arms and crimes ought to be punishable by death.

From a biblical perspective, Old Testament laws treat ending a pregnancy (even when it's ended as an act of violence) as much different than murder. And "turn the other cheek" doesn't seem compatible with most NRA slogans. Of course, we have seen so many questionable death penalty verdicts, particularly against poor or underrepresented racial ethnic communities, that any Christian ought to shudder at the thought. Even without judicial system bias, does the death penalty make sense in the light of "love your enemies"?

Of course, this logic doesn't have as much to do with Christianity as it does with something closely related to Christianity: patriarchy. The patriarchal model works when men make the decisions for women. The male will, in return, provide for and protect the female and her offspring. We have many rituals of patriarchy (such as the father "giving" his daughter to be married), and its logic often permeates our society, often without question.

Pro-choice advocates want to take away the decision-making from men and give women the choice. If gun rights and the death penalty are taken away, then that lessens the ability for a man to protect his family. In both situations, patriarchy would be endangered.

Phil Snider

I've always respected the ethical consistency of those who advocate for a seamless garment of life, i.e., those who are pro-life across the board, including opposition to war and the death penalty. Inasmuch as 250 words allow, this reflects the position I hold today (if I had more words I'd add a few nuances).

In order to make sense of the incongruities harbored in this question, theorists point out that some who support things like the death penalty or war yet oppose abortion do so because unborn babies are innocent, whereas those sentenced to the death penalty, or those who are victims of war, are not innocent. Yet even this line of thought fails to recognize that no small percentage of those on death row are wrongly accused, and that the number of civilians killed in war often exceeds the number of soldiers killed, all of which should give us pause.

Moreover, any ethic that claims to be pro-life must be concerned about caring for babies even, and especially, after they are born. Numerous studies show that if a society truly wants to reduce the number of abortions, then reducing the rate of poverty is essential. It's hypocritical, as John Caputo notes, "to populate the killing fields of poverty by aligning oneself with, or even remaining silent about, policies that exacerbate economic and social injustice, which seed and cultivate the fields of abortion... [T]he right to life spans the entire spectrum and it includes not only fetuses but felons, not only friends but enemies, 'from womb to tomb.'"

· ·

Sean Gladding

A. This question describes the views of some of my friends who see themselves as being "pro-life," a position which I suspect the questioner in this case would see as being problematic. Here is how they have explained their views to me. God is the giver of life, and we are called to protect human life, especially that of those who cannot protect themselves, most obviously the unborn. Hence, owning and being willing to use a weapon to defend human life is consistent with being pro-life, even if the aggressor is killed in the process. The death penalty for murder is, in their opinion, both sanctioned by scripture and is the ultimate expression of belief in the sanctity of human life. They see these beliefs as being consistently pro-life, which is the point at which I disagree.

Regardless of whether we believe the death penalty as it is practiced in the U.S. is a deterrent against murder (it is not), or is applied justly (it is not), every time we take a life, we are enacting the belief that this person's life is irredeemable, that forgiveness and reconciliation are impossible, and/or that this life is less valuable than others, all of which deny the power and work of Christ, who, lest we forget, was himself executed by the State. If we are going to be against abortion, let us also be pro-life following birth, striving to provide for all children the abundant life Jesus promised.

· · · · · ·

Scriptural reference(s):

Genesis 9:6; Exodus 20:1–17; Exodus 21:12; Exodus 21:22–25; Matthew 5:39–46; Romans 13:1–4

Suggested additional sources:

- *Whose Freedom? The Battle over American's Most Important Idea* by George Lakoff
- *The Political Mind: A Cognitive Scientist's Guide to Your Brain and Its Politics* by George Lakoff
- *God's Politics: Why the Right Gets It Wrong and the Left Doesn't Get It* by Jim Wallis
- *The Death Penalty Debate* by H. Wayne House and John Howard Yoder
- http://www.amnesty.org/en/death-penalty
- *Dead Man Walking*, movie

Questions for further discussion/thought:

1 .What do you think about abortion, the death penalty, and gun laws?
2. Do you think that the particular stances that some Christians take have more to do with politics, patriarchy, or the Bible?
3. According to studies, you are far more likely to be killed by a gun if you own a gun. Why do you think this is the case?
4. What does "pro-life" mean for you? How did you come to that understanding?
5. Do you have friends who think differently than you about this? How can you engage in constructive conversation with each other?

Source cited:

- *What Would Jesus Deconstruct?* by John Caputo (Grand Rapids, Mich.: Baker Academic, 2007)

Many Christians describe themselves as "evangelical." What does that mean? Is that the same as being conservative?

....

Andrew Marin

A I consider myself an evangelical. The problem with that word is a vocal cross-section of self-proclaiming evangelicals who see it as their only job to make others have "correct" theological and political beliefs. This has led to the confusion of the definition.

I believe reclaiming the word *evangelical* starts with how Christians view their call by Jesus in Matthew 28 as the Great Commission. Living in the Great Commission doesn't mean it will ever turn into the Great Reality. There will always be an "other," an opposite—those who will never believe, be on our side, or agree with who we are, and what we're all about. OK. Now that we've got that out of the way, the main question is: What do we do with "those" people? The answer should be the job of the evangelical. Here is my brief starting point:

The struggle for any label is both clumsy and backward because inherent to labels are issues of branding, access, and the potential privilege that comes with "correct" associations with said label. I am Andrew, a man who loves progressives and conservatives and works with both while faithfully seeking to establish the Kingdom here on earth as it is in heaven. What happens from that work of faithfulness is not my business. Rather, it is a challenge to me to see if I actually do believe what the Bible says, that it's the Holy Spirit's job to convict, God's job to judge, and mine to love.

Carol Howard Merritt: About twenty years ago, I was a conservative Christian. (Since then, my views have changed.) We called ourselves "fundamentalists" and were proud that we held to the five fundamentals of the faith (six-day creation, virgin birth, substitutionary atonement, Christ's divinity, and hell). Soon historians like Martin E. Marty and Scott Appleby began to link the word "fundamentalism" to Jewish and Muslim people. Fundamentalism quickly dropped out of favor as a term, but the litmus test of belief still remains strong.

When Charismatic, nondenominational, and Bible-believing Baptist congregations became more organized in their political action, they needed a label to express to the media, donors, and politicians who they were and how their constituents represented a growing force. "Evangelical" fit nicely. It was a historic word and it has two Greek roots meaning "good" and "messenger," so it highlights the importance of spreading the gospel. People like Jerry Falwell could suddenly get face time on CNN, not because he was the founder of a small Christian college, but because he spoke for millions, he spoke for the "Evangelicals."

Now sociologists label people in terms of "evangelical" in order to designate conservative Christian groups. But most labels get muddy as they try to tidy up a messy reality. "Evangelical" also has historic resonance for many in liberal denominational churches; in fact, one of the major progressive denominations is the Evangelical Lutherans. Many people in historically liberal denominations consider themselves to be evangelical. And there are many liberal or progressive Christians who are also evangelical.

·······························
Matthew Paul Turner

When I was in my twenties, a very gentle pastor taught me that "to be an evangelical" means "you're a follower of Jesus, one who embraces the teachings of Christ, one who engages God through Jesus and community." He also taught me that to be "evangelical" means that you are one who pursues loving the poor, showing compassion to widows, and believing that the last truly are the first.

But his definition did not match the one I heard Christians and non-Christians in media use. They downsized the definition to reflect people who were "conservative" or "biblical" in their views on politics, social issues, and morality. Rarely was Jesus mentioned.

In 2006, I called that old pastor friend of mine to ask a question. "Does 'being evangelical' mean that I have to also be a conservative?" I said.

He laughed. "Who the hell told you that? Being evangelical means you're kind, compassionate, and hope-filled. You can do that and be conservative or liberal."

So, as self-proclaiming evangelical, I don't believe that "evangelical" is a synonym for "conservative." For me, it means I am passionate about the things of Jesus, knowing those things, doing those things, hoping those things, and trying my best to live those things.

· · · · · ·

Scriptural reference(s):

Matthew 22:36–40; Acts 17:11; Romans 14:10–12

Suggested additional sources:

- *The King Jesus Gospel* by Scot McKnight
- *With* by Skye Jethani
- *The Reason for God* by Timothy Keller

- *Fundamentalisms Observed* by Martin E. Marty and R. Scott Appleby
- *The Fall of the Evangelical Nation* by Christine Wicker

Questions for further discussion/thought:

1. Do you know "evangelicals" who look, think, and act differently? What draws you to each?
2. Do you think Jesus would have labeled himself as an evangelical?
3. How do you understand the term "evangelical"?
4. Do you think of the term in a historic, theological, or political sense?
5. Once politicians and the larger society adopt a term, do you believe that the historic sense can still apply, or does it lose its meaning?

Source cited:

- *What Is an Evangelical?* by Andrew Marin, (http://sojo.net/blogs/2011/10/24/andrew-marin-answers-what-evangelical)

Do Christians still believe that wives should submit to their husbands? What do they mean by "submit"?

....
Margot Starbuck

The stereotype of those who favor the submission of wives to husbands, and women to men, can elicit images of creepy Stepford Wives and women in church with duct tape over their mouths. To be fair, though, Christians who maintain women's submission usually have something less evil in mind. These would suggest that men have a God-given authority, and responsibility, as heads of household and leaders over women.

Many others, like me, and also my husband, believe that, in Christ, the former distinctions and hierarchies between Jew and Greek, slave and free, male and female have been erased (Gal. 3:28). As it was in the beginning (Gen. 1:26–27), the image of God is reflected in both male and female.

The temptation for folks like me, though, is to throw the baby out with the bathwater. Specifically, because of the historic ways the word "submit" has been abused, we're tempted to scrap it altogether both in our vocabulary and also in our relationships. The fact is, Paul's teaching on submission has a lot more to say to husbands than it does to wives! Husbands, said Paul, are to love their wives the way Christ loved the church. That Christ died for the church makes me, as a woman, actually suspect I got the better deal! Marriages do thrive when, in humility, love, and service, wives and husbands submit to one another.

....
Andrew Marin

When I asked my wife about this question, she responded with, "Phhhh. They better not believe that anymore." I guess that's the answer in my marriage.

Theologically, the New Testament uses the word "submit" and its variations seventy-six times, with no one escaping its inclusion, even as far as Jesus' unenthusiastic submission to the will of God for his death.

As for the particular passage in question (Eph. 5:22–23), it's important to note that the literal Greek can be translated, "Wives, to your husbands as to the Lord" (v. 22). The Greek for "to submit" is absent from the original text. This shows that verse 21, then, is a transitional statement of submission, whose broader context includes Christ, wives, husbands, and the Church (vv. 21–33).

If both husbands and wives are to submit to, and love each other as to the Lord, a free-will submission is being described. The Lord does not make anyone submit; it's a choice we all have to make. Therefore, just the same occurs in a marriage relationship, both partners must choose to submit to each other out of love and reverence.

Finally, Paul is writing in a context where men were culturally and religiously dominant over women and the family. Though the exact term in verse 23 is translated as "head," that is bound by specific words in time and place. The overarching principle of mutuality in submission by husbands, wives, and Christ throughout the larger passage is what transculturally applies to contemporary society.

....

Jonathan Brooks

A. This verse is found in Ephesians chapter 5 and is meant to be a liberating passage for women who were treated as property. The original Greek word translated here as "submit" is more accurately translated as "attached to or identified with," and Paul was addressing the fact that women, even after being married, could still be identified with their fathers (if brought back home at least twice a year), and thus their endowments and property could continue to be held by the father. This is why Paul later quotes Genesis when he says a man should *leave* his father and mother and be joined to his wife (Eph. 5:31, referring to Gen. 2:42). The passage begins with the words "submit yourselves one to another" and is followed by the command for husbands to love their wives as Christ loved the church (Eph. 5:25). The passage is also translated using the word "head" to represent the man's relationship to the woman and Christ's relationship to man. The Greek word originally used there is actually better translated as "source." It actually reads that man is the source of woman and Christ the source of man. Similar to the head of a river being its source, this refers to the Christian view that Eve was taken from the rib of Adam. The verse is about the way Christ loves the church and is not at all about husbands' supremacy over wives. It is a liberating passage that puts more pressure on husbands to treat their wives with great respect and to love them as Christ loves the church.

• • • • • •

Scriptural reference(s):

Genesis 1:26–27; Matthew 26:42; Galatians 3:28; Ephesians 5:21–33

Suggested additional sources:

- *Choose Love Not Power* by Tony Campolo
- *Four Views on Free Will* by John Martin Fischer, Robert Kane, Derk Pereboom and Manuel Vargas
- *Hard Saying of the Bible* by Walter C. Kaiser Jr., Peter H. Davids, F.F. Bruce, and Manfred T. Brauch
- *Did St. Paul get Jesus Right?* By David Wenham
- *Christians for Biblical Equality* http://www.cbeinternational.org/
- *Christian Feminism Today*: http://www.eewc.com/
- *Gender and Grace* by Mary Stewart Van Leeuwen

Questions for further discussion/thought:

1. How do you look at your spouse—in mutuality, through the lens of submission, or a combination of both?
2. How does the view of your spouse influence your relationship with the Lord and the Church?
3. In a marital relationship, what would mutual submission look like to you?
4. Which do you think is more difficult: submission or unconditional love?
5. Take a stab at defending the position you do not hold. If you're an egalitarian, can you think of any legit reasons others might hold another position?

Source cited:

- *The Holy Bible*

Is the Christian God the same God as the God of Islam and Judaism? If not, what's the difference? If so, why have three separate religions?

······················

Bart Campolo

A. I think a better question might be whether the Gods of any two writers in this book are the same, or whether the God of John Piper is the same God as the God of Rob Bell, or, while you're at it, whether Paul's God was the same as Matthew's, or Mark's, or Luke's, or John's. The answer, of course, all depends on your point of view.

From their perspective, all of my friends and relatives would say that they know the same Bart Campolo, and on one level they would all be right. On another level, however, each one of them has a different understanding of who I am, how I think, and what I want.

Part of that is because I have gotten to know each of them in different ways, under different circumstances, and at different levels of intensity. Another part, of course, is that each of them is at a different place in his or her life, with different capacities and different needs, which causes me to share myself with them differently. A final part, I'm afraid, is that some of them are morons who totally misunderstand me no matter how hard I try to set them straight.

There's only one God, I think, and we've all got that God wrong in our own way. Let's just hope Jesus was right about all that grace.

······················

Hugh Hollowell

A. The other two religions seem to think so. The prophet Mohammed was sure he was worshiping the same god the Jews and Christians were (see, for example, Qur'an 29:46), and the apostles thought they were worshiping the same god Moses and Abraham knew. Both Arab Muslims and Arab Christians pray to Allah, which is just the Arabic word for God, and Spanish Muslims, Christians, and Jews all pray to Dios, the Spanish name for God. The English word "god" is probably less than 800 years old.

They all worship the same God. Where they differ is how they think this God is decisively known. Jews think God is known by the covenants God has made, Muslims think God is known through the Koran, and Christians believe God is known through the person of Jesus. One God, three religions.

Two Friars and a Fool

From God's point of view, yes. If we trust that there is a real God who exists outside our imagination, then that God is really out there somewhere, and human longing is aimed at that God one way or another. There is not a God competition where the weakest God is voted off the island. There's just God, and our incomplete attempts to understand.

From the point of view of the various faiths that profess belief in a God, though, we have to say no. Christianity, Judaism, and Islam ask different questions and come to different answers. It is a little bit disrespectful, if you think about it, to say that "we all believe in the same God," or that these three faiths can be described with the bland term "Abrahamic." There's a lot more than Abraham going on in Christianity, Judaism, and Islam, including significant disagreements both on details and on big themes.

These differences freak some people out in each of the three traditions, but we wouldn't expect it to be any other way. We have an infinite, transcendent God, who literally embodies mystery, breaking into our human experience in various ways. These differing experiences of God will lead to differences in understanding, language, and practices. Christian scripture is an ongoing argument between voices that disagree on significant questions. This just mirrors our experience in the world. Out of all this dealing with real differences, we come to understand more about God and ourselves, not less.

• • • • • •

Suggested additional sources:

- http://www.patheos.com/Library/Islam.html
- http://www.patheos.com/Library/Judaaism.html
- http://www.huffingtonpost.com/charles-kimball/whither-the-clash-of-civi_b_823631.html
- *Allah: A Christian Response* by Miroslav Volf
- *The World Religions* by Huston Smith

Questions for further discussion/thought:

1. What beliefs or practices of another religion are you curious about? What beliefs or practices do you engage in that someone of another religion may be curious about?

2. In many Western societies right now, we are hearing more and more about a "clash of civilizations," often with one side identified as Christian or "Judeo-Christian" and, on the other side, Islam. What possibilities exist between this so-called "clash of civilizations" on the one hand and the idea that "all Abrahamic religions are basically the same" on the other?

What do Christians believe happens after they die, and why? Do they believe they are judged immediately and are ferried off to heaven or hell? What about purgatory?

....

Phil Snider

According to the churches I grew up in, those who accept Jesus as their Lord during their lifetime go to heaven. Those who don't go to hell. It's pretty cut and dry. Once this eternal destination is determined, it's irrevocable.

Christians from more liberal traditions aren't quite as certain. Some view heaven as the place where they will reconnect with loved ones, while others see it as a metaphor for the renewal of creation in which God's justice and peace is fully realized.

Few liberals believe in a literal hell where souls are tormented forever. For them, this makes God out to be a cosmic torturer that has much more in common with ruthless tyrants than with Jesus Christ. While this can lead fundamentalists to criticize liberals for not taking God's judgment into proper consideration, liberals agree that actions do have consequences. Not taking care of the environment, for instance, will one day make the earth uninhabitable for human beings. Telling people they will go to hell if they are gay can lead to lifetimes of depression and loneliness. Beginning a war casually can lead to the annihilation of untold thousands of people.

Most Christians agree that actions have consequences. But when the point of Christianity is reduced to going to heaven when we die, the consequences of our actions in this world, of living and loving, of caring and giving, are actually diminished. When Christianity is watered down only to securing one's place in the afterlife, this can lead to, as Peter Rollins notes, "nothing less than a form of nihilism, for the belief in the eternal life [robs] this life of its fragile, fleeting beauty." This isn't to deny the afterlife, but to say that many Christians, including myself, are more interested in life *before* death than life after death.

....

Matthew Paul Turner

Christians believe all kinds of things about what happens after we die. While I find some ideas to be more compelling than others, all of us are essentially guessing. In the New Testament we do get vague references to resurrection (in contrast to a purely spiritual afterlife), and an insistence that God is "restoring all things" and "making all things new." However, what happens to people who die in the interim is a question that the Bible only addresses indirectly with a handful of dissonant hints. Some parts of scripture imply a sort of awareness, while others seem to indicate something like sleep. Jesus offers a weird parable about a rich jerk and a poor guy named Lazarus, from which some have constructed detailed explanations of what happens after we die. Unfortunately, parables don't tend to work like that, and although the ending seems to be heavily modified by Jesus, the plot appears to be a popular parable in circulation at the time, which isn't original to Jesus.

Some speculate that "time" is a part of the created order and, therefore, God and God's "realm" exist outside of time. In their view, this renders the question somewhat moot, since it removes any interim time period between now and God's ultimate future for those who have died. I like that. Some argue that our loved ones who have died are conscious in the presence of God and are watching over us in some sense. I like that, too. Some argue that the consciousness of those who have died is resting until God fulfills his promises about reconciliation and the restoration of all things. There are days when I find that scenario very appealing as well. The truth is that when it comes to the specifics of what happens after we die, we're basically guessing and hoping. We're in good company, though, because people have been doing this since the beginning of time. However, I am convinced of this: God, who is most clearly seen in Jesus, is love, and God promises that death doesn't have the last word. Love does. I can live with that.

. . . .

Bart Campolo

Christians believe all kinds of things about the afterlife, but almost all of them believe there is one. I used to think it was a package deal: if you believed in God, then you must believe in the immortality of your own soul, too. And so I did, or at least so I told myself. While heaven and hell had nothing to do with my reasons for becoming a Christian, it literally went without saying that accepting Jesus as my personal Savior meant accepting that such eternal destinations actually existed. It never occurred to me that someone might put their faith in the living God without believing something awaits us beyond the day we die. It only occurs to me now, I think, because I am well on my way to being that someone.

I am no neuroscientist, but I have studied enough to know that each of the many and various parts of my personality has a physical location in my brain, and that if and when that location is altered in some way, my personality will be altered as well. Stimulate my limbic system one way, and

I will become more sexually aggressive. Stimulate it a different way and I will become depressed. Damage part of my amygdala and I will become unable to form loving relationships. Damage part of my prefrontal cortex, on the other hand, and I will lose all sense of right and wrong.

In other words, my brain and my soul are essentially one and the same thing. My individual identity is a particular arrangement of particular organic matter over a particular period of time, and when that period comes to an end, that matter will be rearranged into something (or perhaps someone) else. So then, when my ashes return to ashes, and my dust to dust, I reckon Bart Campolo will be no more.

And yet, just as I still believe in a living God, I still believe in eternal life and daily strive toward that goal. I very intentionally love and teach as many children and young adults as I can, trusting that by so doing I become a small part of each one, even as my parents and best teachers became part of me. In this way, I hope to live on through their lives even after I die, and then in the lives of the younger ones they teach and love. As long as that line goes on, I believe, so will I. Even so, my personal immortality is not the point.

The point is that, as one who has so deeply appreciated my own human experience, I am desperate to ensure endless generations have that experience as well. I cannot breathe forever, but this air is so sweet that I want someone to breathe it always. I want someone, many someones, to taste this wonderful food, and to savor this fabulous wine. Having family and friends has been such a joy to me, laughing and dancing and making love have been so delightful, working to exhaustion and then resting has been so satisfying, and raising children so terrifying, believing in God so inspiring, and aging so interesting, that I can't stand the thought that people might cease to do those things. I love life, after all, not just my own life.

Striving toward eternal life, for me at least, is not so much about getting God to punch my ticket for heaven as it is about doing all I can to ensure that humanity itself endures, and in particular that best part of humanity, which scripture calls the "Image of God." It is about asking Grace to guide my thoughts and actions, to literally flow through me into the lives of those who are growing up behind me. It is about keeping the faith by loving my neighbor, and trusting that both of us are thereby becoming part of God's endless love.

· · · · · · · · · · · · · · · ·

Doug Pagitt

A Christians have held wildly different views of judgment and afterlife narratives. It is my view that we should understand all the Bible's description of afterlife not as a step-by-step process of what someone will experience as some sort of "five steps to getting your driver's license at the DMV and what to expect when you arrive" listing. Rather, we are to see this language as poetic description of how God brings about righteousness in the world. It is a genre of colorful, big themes of God's work in all creation. Too often people go into the text as if with a scalpel and pull out certain phrases and notions to use literally. God will recreate all of heaven and earth in a much bigger and more beautiful sense than our explanations can ever provide.

Strangely, for all the things the Bible says and all that Christian tradition teaches on so many matters, there is no account from someone who has died to tell us what happens with life. We have no authority on which to speak on these topics. We simply don't know, and have never known. And this limited information has served as "good enough" for billions of people. There is no need to try and overly specify what we can only guess about. Everyone is piecing afterlife explanations together, and this should compel us to hold our views very loosely.

· · · · · ·

Scriptural reference(s):

1 Corinthians 15:22; 1 Timothy 4:10

Suggested additional sources:

- *Love Wins* by Rob Bell
- *What Does the Bible Really Say about Hell?* by Randolph Klassen
- *Surprised by Hope* by N.T. Wright

Questions for further discussion/thought:

1. Do you think Christianity should place more emphasis on heaven or on earth?
2. Do you think Jesus understood his death and resurrection as a necessary transaction so that we could go to heaven?

Source cited:

- *The Fidelity of Betrayal* by Peter Rollins (Brewster, Mass.: Paraclete Press, 2008)

To be a Christian, is it necessary to believe that Jesus really (as in factually) healed the blind, made the lame to walk, rose from the dead, and ascended into somewhere called heaven, where he sits with someone he calls his Father? And if not, why do Christians recite a creed that says that?

Adam J. Copeland

A. Years ago a good friend of mine went through some of the most horrible personal tragedies you can imagine. Through it all, he kept attending church regularly, choosing to sit alone in the balcony. At one point I asked my friend how he was doing with his faith. I wondered how all his struggles had affected him.

My friend told me that there were many Sundays when he woke up and going to church was the last thing he wanted to do. He was angry at God, wrestling with deep questions and wavering belief. But, most Sundays, he did eventually make it to worship.

"On those Sundays," he said, "the most meaningful part of the service is always the Creed. When I am struggling so much with my faith, it's essential for me to hear the faith of the church. When I can't say the words, the church believes for me."

Belief is a funny thing. When my friend stood to hear the Creed recited, part of him knew it was true, or *needed* it to be true, even as he struggled to say the words himself.

As he questioned in his deep grief, did my friend ever cease to be a Christian? I think that's the wrong direction of consideration. Instead, I wonder, *How can the faith of the church support and sustain us in our questions and longing for answers? What power do the stories of Jesus' miracles, death, and Resurrection have for those who long to believe?*

Hugh Hollowell

A. I don't think so. (I know good people who disagree with me on this, however.) But even if you don't buy all the claims of historic

Christianity, you can still recite the creeds. By way of illustration: If you live in the United States, odds are you have recited the pledge of allegiance to the flag. You probably had no problem doing so. Yet, even the most fervent patriot will agree that we are not "one nation under God, indivisible, with liberty and justice for all." Yet, we say the pledge anyway.

Sharing a creed unites Christians, just like the pledge unites Americans. And while there may not be liberty and justice for all, at our core, the hope of that is what drives the idea of being American. And I may not "believe" that Jesus will come again to judge the wicked and reward the faithful, but the dream of that binds me to the historic faith and to the faithful.

So, I think of it as sort of like the pledge: I don't think it is all going to happen, but I sure hope it does. And saying the creeds in worship binds me with others who hope it does, too.

· · · · · · · · · · · · · · · · ·

Phil Snider

The vast majority of mainstream biblical scholars emphasize that the Bible doesn't have to be taken literally in order to be taken seriously. This doesn't diminish the value of the Bible, but increases it all the more. The Bible is full of figurative language—parables, narratives, allegories, metaphors, and so on—that operate on a variety of different levels. The more we recognize the poetic quality of religious language, including historic creeds, the more we recognize the enduring value of religion.

Religion is true in the same way that a poem or piece of art is true. To borrow the words of John Caputo: "By the 'religious' I do not mean some preternatural event in a Stephen King novel, or even an extraordinary visitation by a supernatural being like an angel. Of course, that is exactly what Luke's story of the Annunciation to Mary was, but that is a function of great religious narratives, in which we find human experience writ large, the defining features of our life magnified in moving and unforgettable stories, in brilliant religious figures."

Experiencing the meaning and depth of Charles Dickens' *A Christmas Carol* doesn't require that you believe in ghosts from the past, present, and future. Neil Gaiman, paraphrasing the great Christian writer G. K. Chesterton, said it best: "Fairy Tales are more than true; not because they tell us that dragons exist, but because they tell us that dragons can be defeated."

· · · · · ·

Scriptural reference(s):

Luke 1:26–27; Hebrews 11:1; 1 Corinthians 13:12

Suggested additional sources:

- *A Good Man Is Hard to Find (Short Story)* by Flannery O'Connor
- *The Heart of Christianity* by Marcus Borg
- *On Religion* by John Caputo

Questions for further discussion/thought:

1. Our modern post-enlightenment understanding of miracles is very different from that of other ages. For you, what is more powerful: facts or stories?
2. What matters more: Christian beliefs or Christian actions?
3. If religion is true in the way that a poem or piece of art is true, how does this influence the way you read the Bible? The way you worship? The way you pray?

Source cited:

- *On Religion* by John Caputo (London; New York: Routledge, 2001)

Why is the church growing in Africa and Asia, but declining in Europe and the U.S.?

....

Adam J. Copeland

Complicated factors are at work in global church growth and decline, many of which are cultural. For instance, much of the West's scientific rationalist approach to life makes a false dichotomy between science and religion. If the cultural norms say that curious, open-minded people cannot be Christian, then the church will certainly falter. Along those same lines, some people mistakenly believe we have evolved past a time when we need religion, as if technological progress can replace God, sin, and death.

We are also at a time in the West when, for believers and nonbelievers, the church is often less than compelling. When pastors ride around in Bentleys, and many denominations debate human sexuality more than how to end poverty, the church certainly could be cited as the cause of its own decline.

My stream of the Christian tradition emphasizes that it's the work of the Holy Spirit that grows the church rather than primarily efforts of our own. Perhaps the Spirit, then, is particularly primed to work in Africa and Asia, where God's good news might feel more immanent, powerful, and life-changing.

Before you jump to the conclusion that the Spirit has stopped working in Europe and the U.S., however, consider another possibility. Perhaps it's those of us in Europe and the U.S. who have abandoned God, not the other way around.

....

Phil Jackson

Churches in Europe and the U.S. are dry and lifeless. Let's just be real and call it what it is. There is not a sense of urgency for God that fuels the passion to serve in powerful ways. The church in America is simply tolerated, but not celebrated as a force for God to build His Kingdom.

The churches in Africa, Asia, and elsewhere are often serving from places of suffering. Often there are threats of persecution if they share with others about their faith in Jesus, or even have a church service. If you have ever been in a situation where you were suffering or in place of urgency for your life, you understand the desire of people in these other countries to passionately seek help from anywhere, looking for a miracle. The Church in the U.S. has stopped looking for anything except air conditioning in the summer, heat in the winter, and a funny yet comfortable sermon that makes them feel good.

The church in America has been hijacked from Jesus by politics and prosperity Gospel that have all sought to keep things safe for those who attend their church. This is not what Christ has called us to be; we are to help invoke God's Kingdom here on earth, yet the church in America has overlooked so many issues of injustice, morality, care for the poor, and generally has settled for a Christ without suffering.

Churches in the U.S. have lost our toughness. We have mistakenly come to believe that church is a place to be comfortable, rather than being a place of constant struggle for justice. There's a lot we can learn from our Christian brothers and sisters on other continents.

• • • • • •

Scriptural reference(s):

Matthew 25:40; Matthew 22:36-40; Matthew 28:16-20; Acts 2:37–42

Suggested additional sources:

- *The Next Christendom: The Coming of Global Christianity* by Philip Jenkins
- *Living for Jesus without Embarrassing God* by Tony Campolo

Questions for further discussion/thought:

1. If you were God, would you grow the church evenly around the world or not?
2. What are the signs of healthy church growth?
3. What in your community doesn't reflect your understanding of God's Kingdom? What more can you do to be Jesus in that area and to help God's Kingdom come?

Why is personal/individual salvation emphasized so much more in modern Christianity than global transformation of the world into the just peace realm of God's commonwealth? How can one person be saved while others continue to suffer?

. . . .
Adam J. Copeland

A. One way to get at this question is through that old favorite verse, John 3:16: "For God so loved the world that he gave his only Son, so that everyone who believes in him may not perish but may have eternal life" (NRSV). This verse is often used in an exclusive way to emphasize the need for personal acceptance of Jesus' love.

There's nothing wrong with mentioning God's love for individuals, but the Greek word that is translated "world" has very corporate shades to it. The word *cosmos* means not "church" or "the people" but "the whole of creation." The emphasis is that God loves all that God has created: you and me, the fields and the fawns, and even (especially?) the world that is alienated from God.

Perhaps our personal/individual approach to faith is connected to the American work ethic that emphasizes personal responsibility. We value individual rights and personal freedom, so much so, in fact, that we forget God necessarily calls us to relationship with others, living out our faith in a world that is all God's to begin with.

With a view toward this more corporate nature of the faith, salvation expands far beyond an individual concern. Salvation is not about what happens to individual souls, but a corporate concern regarding God's whole creation—including people, the earth, and even all life.

. . . .
Matthew Paul Turner

A. Perspective is everything here. For those of us in contemporary Western Christianity, our thinking about personal salvation is probably due to the fact that we've been so thoroughly converted to consumerism that we approach everything from that understanding. If we're in the market for some spirituality, we look for the best purveyor of religious goods and services for the lowest cost in terms of time, money, etc. As good consumers, we look for a place (that's right, a church that is primarily a "place" rather than a community) that meets our felt-needs and desires. Unfortunately, churches for the most part have embraced their role in this particular understanding, and they tend to market a gospel to the individual consumer accordingly.

Interestingly enough, in both the Old and New Testaments, the word that is most often translated "salvation" literally means "rescue." I've come to believe that the Christian concept of salvation is rooted in the ancient Jewish concept of *Shalom*, which means something akin to "harmony" between God and people, harmony between people and other people, and harmony between people and God's creation. The assumption is that harmony was broken, chaos is wreaking havoc, but God is reconciling creation back into harmony. God is rescuing us from chaos and fragmentation. Salvation by definition cannot be merely a personal experience. It is inherently relational. Moreover, salvation is not a commodity to be possessed. Those who are being reconciled also become agents of reconciliation. Those who have been rescued by God become agents of salvation. It's not that you "have" salvation. It's that salvation has you.

Phil Snider

A. Martin Luther King Jr. once said, "Any religion that professes to be concerned with the souls of men and is not concerned with the slums that damn them, the economic conditions that strangle them and the social conditions that cripple them is a dry-as-dust religion," functioning as "an opiate of the people." I couldn't agree more.

I don't understand how a heavenly paradise can be experienced as anything less than hell if one of my loved ones is suffering, unless while in heaven I could somehow find a way not to care about their fate, which basically goes against everything I've ever been taught about Christian ethics.

We frequently use religion as a means of escaping the world, for the same reasons we might be drawn to drugs or alcohol. We don't want to face the trauma and struggle and heartache that often accompany life, so we repress it as much we can. We have personal problems we want God to fix, whether now or in the afterlife. Yet at its most profound level Christianity isn't about escaping the trauma that marks our lives by isolating into individualized shells, but rather is about entering into the dark night of the soul together, facing it head on, with the same honesty that Christ displayed on the cross when crying out, "My God, my God, why have you forsaken me?"

It is when we let go of God as the means of escaping the world that we find God.

....

Sean Gladding

One answer to the question is that we have been shaped far more by our culture than by the Story of God that we have received in scripture. There is little question that the U.S. is a radically individualistic and increasingly narcissistic culture. Growing up, my favorite chocolate bar was Twix: "made for sharing." But by the late '90s the advertising was, "Two for me, none for you." We have done the same with John 3:16. "For God so loved the world…," the world ("*cosmos*") referring to all that God has created. Now we read it as meaning the collection of individuals who are going to heaven while the world burns.

But is it fair to lay the blame entirely at the feet of culture? Perhaps not. If I think the problem of sin is that I am going to hell, rather than its effect on the entirety of creation, then once I am "saved," all I really need to do is wait to die and tell others that they too can go to heaven. It allows resourced suburban churches to bus poor kids out of my neighborhood for "church" on Sundays, and then drop them off afterward rather than entering the world of their poverty.

I wonder if we do not want the transforming Story of God's kingdom coming, because that would mean having to "work out [our] salvation with fear and trembling" (Phil. 2:12b, NIV). It's much easier to invite Jesus into my heart, and wait to go to heaven.

• • • • • •

Scriptural reference(s):

Psalm 139:8; Matthew 27:46; John 3:16; Romans 8:19–22; Romans 12:15; Philippians 2:1–13

Suggested additional sources:

- *Hope in the Lord Jesus Christ,* a PC(USA) study paper available for download http://www.pcusa.org/resource/hope-lord-jesus-christ/
- *Stride Toward Freedom* by Martin Luther King Jr.
- *Insurrection: To Believe Is Human; to Doubt Divine* by Peter Rollins

- *The Hole in Our Gospel* by Richard Stearns
- *Velvet Elvis* by Rob Bell
- *The Last Word and the Word after That* by Brian McLaren
- *Salvation Means Creation Healed* by Howard Snyder

Questions for further discussion/thought:

1. Is Christianity as individualistic in other societies?
2. How would you describe salvation?
3. Most of us have felt abandoned by God at some point along the way. Have you ever thought about this as a point of identification with Christ, instead of being contrary to Christ?
4. What is your understanding of "salvation"?
5. Has it changed over the years, and, if so, why and how?
6. How does that shape the way you live your day-to-day life?

Sources cited:

- *The Holy Bible*
- *Stride Toward Freedom* by Martin Luther King Jr. (New York, Harper, 1958), p. 23
- www.Facebook.com/Twix.us

Why do so many evangelicals seem to feel the term "social justice" is a bad thing? Why is it generally associated with leftist political activism?

Andrew Marin

Since the invention of language there have been random terms hijacked from one group, opposing another, for political or theological reasons. No word or phrase has inherent value. The values placed on words are socially constructed to serve a purpose. In most cases that purpose has to do with either power or fear mongering—which is still rooted in an attempt to gain power. To vilify a word, phrase, people group, or belief system is the easiest way to rally people around a cause. That is as true today as it was in the Bible.

In regards to "social justice," the rise of the evangelical prostitution of political conservatism caused "social justice" to become an easy target to push a Republican "Christian" agenda catering to the wealthy capitalist more than the poor who are systemically abused by those wealthy capitalists. Theologically, Jesus talks more about justice and protection for the poor than any other topic, which aligns very closely with a social justice ideology.

Yet the convergence of politics, religion, and power has intermarried itself into a nasty incestuous muck, currently unable to reclaim any distinguishable markings that differentiate one term from the next. It is going to take a new set of terms, ones backed up by actions of reconciliatory agents focused on culturally, socially, theologically, and politically pursuing that which is disconnected, to even begin instilling a change of consciousness toward a new understanding of political and religious engagement toward the other.

Phil Shepherd, *a.k.a.* The Whiskey Preacher

One part of flying I hate the most is short layovers. Your plane arrives late, there's no time to use a real bathroom that's not the size of a dollhouse, you're rushing to the next gate that's always on the opposite side of the terminal (it's never a pretty sight to watch a stout man run in cowboy boots in the middle of an airport), and you certainly don't get the chance to people watch, which is one of my favorite things to do when traveling. Short layovers are the worst. I try to avoid them as much as possible.

As a former evangelical myself, it's been my experience that evangelicals view their time here on earth as a short layover in the grand scheme of things. Heaven is the final destination and things that concern us here on earth, such as social justice, are a distraction from the greater prize. Anything that takes away from the "personal relationship" with Jesus is viewed as a sin in itself. Social justice is seen as a distraction created by liberals who really don't believe in Jesus and heaven. At least that's what I was taught for many years.

For many of us who could consider ourselves post-evangelicals, we have changed our perspective from this time on earth as being a short layover to, instead, seeing it as a gift from our Creator. Social justice then is seen as an extension of our relationship with Jesus, not a distraction from it.

· · · · · · · · · · · · · · · · · ·

Phil Jackson

A. I will start off with a great quote from Medea Benjamin that explains what social justice is in order that you can judge for yourself and have a better position of understanding when people talk about it negatively.

Social justice means moving towards a society where all hungry are fed, all sick are cared for, the environment is treasured, and we treat each other with love and compassion. Not an easy goal, for sure, but certainly one worth giving our lives for!

Medea Benjamin is the co-founder of Global Exchange and Code Pink. Who better than followers of Jesus Christ to lead the world in understanding and living out the teachings of Jesus about social justice. One of the core reasons why evangelicals see the term so negatively is that the term has assumed baggage that has hurt the purity of the gospel. What people who take a negative view of the term "social justice" don't understand is that the gospel and social justice are one in the same. If you take either one away, the other is depleted of its power. Jesus taught to love your God with all your heart, soul, and mind, and to love your neighbor as yourself. This is the gospel and social justice all in one. He taught that whatever we do to the least of these is what we do to him! This is just what Medea stated, that social justice is moving toward a society where all are cared for, are treated equally, and treat each other with love and compassion.

· · · · · ·

Scriptural reference(s):

Matthew 22:34–40; Matthew 25:31–46; Matthew 28:11–15; Acts 11:24

Suggested additional sources:

- *Fear* by Joanna Bourke
- *Left, Right & Christ* by Lisa Sharon Harper and D.C. Innes
- *Love without Agenda* by Jimmy Spencer Jr.
- *With Justice for All* by John Perkins
- *The Post-Evangelical* by Dave Tomlinson
- *Everything Must Change: Jesus, Global Crises, and a Revolution of Hope* by Brian McLaren
- *Everyday Justice: The Global Impact of Our Daily Choices* by Julie Clawson
- www.everydayjustice.net
- www.goodandfairclothing.com
- www.Globalexchange.org

Questions for further discussion/thought:

1. Are there certain terms that, when you hear them, automatically bring about negative political thoughts of another people group?
2. What do you think it will take to undo the hate-filled rhetoric of contemporary political culture?
3. How does social justice fit into your theology?
4. Is our time here on earth a short layover, or is there something more to it? If so, what does that look like?
5. Can you have a personal relationship with Jesus and still believe in social justice?
6. What happens to a town, city, or country that does not practice social justice?

Source cited:

- *The Post-Evangelical* by Dave Tomlinson (El Cajon, Calif.: Zondervan/Youth Specialties, 2003)

Many Christians read and study the King James Version of the Bible. Some believe it is the best and most accurate translation there is. Why? Can I read a different translation? What about paraphrases such as The Message?

....
Jonathan Brooks

A. Thou shalt comprehend thine manuscript as paramount as is achievable, and scrutinize the periphery in any manner thusly deemed appropriate. Translation: You can read whichever translation makes it easier for you to comprehend God's word.

Many Christians hold on to one translation even though they find themselves struggling for understanding. I believe the Bible is meant to be read and understood, so it is important that the individual reader finds a version he or she can read and understand. I also believe that the Bible was not written *to* us; it was written *for* us, meaning it was written to an ancient audience, and it is our responsibility to understand that but still use it in our modern culture. It is already difficult to understand some passages because of the cultural differences of our time. Reading paraphrases such as *The Message* and others can be helpful. Translators such as Eugene H. Peterson have gone through serious care to bring an ancient language to a modern audience. I would advise you to have as many translations as possible; this will help you gain different understandings of what the original writers were trying to convey.

....
Sean Gladding

A. The way some people talk about the KJV, one could almost imagine that God should have chosen English for the original version. Its enduring popularity and revered status are quite remarkable given the awkwardness of the way it reads four centuries since it was translated. It was written in order to be read aloud in the liturgy of corporate worship, and the beauty of its poetry still moves us, much as Shakespeare can.

To state that it is the most accurate translation of scripture is to deny 400 years of the expansion of our understanding of both the Hebrew and Greek languages and the cultures out of which the Bible grew. Every translation is already an interpretation, as we choose which words to use from a range of possibilities. To pretend it is not is to be disingenuous. For instance, the translators of the KJV use "prince" for fourteen different Hebrew words. Coincidence? Or because the one paying for their services was King James? The impetus for this third English translation appears to have been the desire to reinforce the established institutional structure of the Church of England, which also no doubt shaped the language used.

When people ask me, "What translation of the Bible should I buy?" I invariably answer, "One you will actually read." This has meant that I often recommend *The Message* version, as it is so accessible for our culture. For me, the question is not which Bible to read, but how to read it. My conviction is that it is to be read in community with others, aloud and often—and then embody what we believe God is saying.

· · · · · · · · · · · · · · · · · · ·

Phil Jackson

The King James Bible uses a linguistic style that no one currently identifies with, yet because of the elegant sound of the words, some folks believe that this is the way we have to talk when speaking to God. There's a lot of information out there about why the King James translation is not necessarily an accurate version of the Bible, and even more information from those who say it is the only version that should be read. So which is it?

If you cannot understand the Word of God, it means nothing. The purest way to read the Bible and to find its deep meaning is to read it in Hebrew, Greek, and/or Aramaic, but this is unrealistic for most of us, just trying to read English. So if you are going to spend time seeking truth from God's Word, find a version that is in a language that you are able to comprehend and to read easily, and go for it!

God is bigger than whatever version you choose, and yet He desires us to know Him though His word. Whether it's a paraphrase or the King James version, we must grow in our understanding of God, and that is best done when we are experiencing Him through His word.

• • • • • •

Scriptural reference(s):

2 Timothy 2:15; 2 Timothy 3:16; Hebrews 4:12

Suggested additional sources:

- *How to Read the Bible for All It's Worth* by Gordon Fee and Douglas Stewart
- *Eat This Book* by Eugene Peterson
- *Manna and Mercy* by Daniel Erlander
- *The Epic of Eden* by Sandra Richter
- *Scripture and the Authority of God: How to Read the Bible Today* by N. T. Wright
- *How to Read the Bible for All Its Worth* by Gordon D. Fee and Douglas Stuart

Questions for further discussion/thought:

1. Can you think of a time when you heard someone incorrectly and it ruined the relationship?
2. How important is it that you truly understand God's commands?
3. If you have read different translations, what was your experience in doing so?
4. What has been your experience of reading the Bible with other people?
5. How has that shaped the way you read the Bible today?
6. Why are there so many different versions of the Bible? Is one better or worse than the other?
7. Why do you think some churches use more than one translation, or even non-literal interpretations of the Bible?

Source cited:

- *The Holy Bible*

What does it actually mean when Christians say they believe that Jesus is the Son of God? And how, if at all, is this different from when other people are called "children of God"?

....

Matthew Paul Turner

Although it is primarily applied to Jesus, the term "Son of God" pops up in other places where it isn't referring to Jesus (and we really wouldn't want it to). For example, in Genesis 6, the "sons of God" apparently thought that the "daughters of men" were hot, so they married them and had some sort of super-babies.

In the New Testament, the term is repeatedly applied to Jesus, and there is an implied exclusiveness to it. Part of the purpose of using this term appears to be subverting the claims of Rome and the Caesars. Beginning with Augustus, many of the Caesars applied the term "son of God" to themselves.

Of course, the most obvious meaning of Jesus as "the Son of God" has to do with the close connection between Jesus and the God he called "Father." This is more striking than it seems. Of the roughly 691 times the word for "father" occurs in the Old Testament, only 13 of them refer to God, and only two people dare to refer to God this way. In contrast, the word for "father" occurs roughly 388 times in the New Testament, and 250 of them refer directly to God, about half of them from Jesus. But, as soon as Jesus makes this seemingly exclusive connection, he deconstructs it, and refers to God as *"our"* Father. In Romans and Galatians, Paul goes on to make the scandalous claim that we have been adopted by God as his children and made co-heirs with Jesus. That isn't just theological jargon. It appears to be relational equality.

....

Phil Snider

It's remarkable how Christian language loses its edge as it's passed down through the centuries. In the early days of Christianity, calling Jesus the "Son of God" was a subversive act, bordering on treason. Why? For one very simple reason: in the Roman Empire, which represented the ruling order of the day, the son of God was Caesar, *not* Jesus. Yet in a sheer act of brilliance, the Christian narratives turned the table of the Roman Empire upside-down. To say that Jesus is the Son of God was to provocatively declare that Caesar is not.

Such rhetoric provided early Christian communities a way of reimagining how they believed God worked, no matter what the dominant powers in place tried to tell them. Is God revealed through brute displays of violence, as with Caesar, or through compassionate love, as with Jesus? Is God revealed through the love of power, as with Caesar, or through the power of love, as with Jesus? The answer to these questions meant the difference between life and death, in more ways than one. Perhaps it still does.

· · · · · · · · · · · · · · · · ·

Doug Pagitt

A. The term "Son of God" was a title, not a description of a relationship. In other words, there is a difference in God's son and the Son of God.

For Jesus and his followers, the term Son of God was connected to the notion of the kingdom of God, which was rich with revolution. The Jews were a minority class under the rule of Rome, and Rome had a very powerful king, Caesar. Caesar declared himself a god. In fact, he declared that he should be referred to as "the son of God." The places in his territory where he was honored as a god were referred to as *ekklesia*, the Greek word that was later used by Christians to refer to the church. Around the empire there were communities that declared the kingdom of Caesar, the son of God, and met in ecclesia for that purpose.

When Jesus declared that the kingdom of God was at hand, it sat in direct contrast to the kingdom of Caesar. It was a political call of how people ought to live in the midst of their world. When the followers of Jesus declared him to be the Son of God, they were doing so in contrast to the claims of the followers of Caesar. This was revolutionary language. So to belong to the kingdom of God was the alternative to belonging to the kingdom of Caesar. This had poignant and dangerous implications.

· · · · · ·

Scriptural reference(s):

Mark 1:1; Mark 15:39

Suggested additional sources:

- *The First Christmas* by Marcus Borg and John Dominic Crossan
- *The Last Week* by Marcus Borg and John Dominic Crossan
- *Re-Imagine the World* by Bernard Brandon Scott

Questions for further discussion/thought:

1. How do most people today think God works? Do you think this is congruent with the way that God worked in the life of Jesus?

2. When it comes to calling Jesus the Son of God, do you think it is more helpful to do so (1) as a form of provocative rhetoric that challenges the dominant power structures of the day or (2) in terms of designating Jesus' divine status as a God?

Do all Christians believe Jesus died for their sins? What exactly does this mean, and where did the belief come from? If some Christians don't believe this, what do they believe about the crucifixion?

....

Bart Campolo

Actually, it has been a long time since I believed the cross, or the Resurrection for that matter, was necessary for our salvation. I know the apostle Paul thinks differently, but on this point I think the apostle Paul, and most of evangelical Christianity, are fundamentally wrong.

As far as I can tell, the essential message of evangelical Christianity is fairly simple: God wants to forgive us, but our sins are so terrible that God must first appease His sense of justice by killing somebody. Jesus, the Son of God, was born of a virgin so that God could kill him instead of us, once and for all, or at least for all who believe.

If I understand Jesus correctly, however, God wants the rest of us to just forgive each other. Not to exact retribution, not to demand compensation, certainly not to kill anybody. Just forgive, plain and simple. And if those same people sin against us again, we're supposed to forgive them again, over and over, out of the goodness of our hearts. You know, seventy times seven times, and all of that.

So, then, it seems to me that if almighty God himself really does want to forgive us, that God must be able to just forgive us in that same way, out of the goodness of God's own heart. At least that's what Jesus suggested when he taught his disciples to pray, "Forgive us our sins, as we forgive those who sin against us"—that is, plainly and simply, without killing anybody.

I don't think Jesus came to deliver us from God, but rather to share God's grace with us, so that we could be delivered from sin itself. God's grace, after all, is what gives us the confidence to overcome everything that is wrong with us, everything that keeps us from him and one another.

Of course, Jesus understood that grace always frightens and infuriates religious leaders, because the notion that God loves and forgives everybody no matter what they do or don't do evacuates the authority of such leaders and their rules. Indeed, Jesus clearly knew in advance that displaying and proclaiming God's grace would get him killed. Getting killed, however, was not the point.

Christian Piatt

In a word, no. The idea that Jesus died for humanity's sins is often called substitutionary atonement. For centuries following the life and death of Jesus, this was not central to the beliefs of many, if not most, Christians. Theologians such as Augustine of Hippo placed a strong emphasis on the salvific importance of the death of Jesus, but before that, most theological thinkers wrote about Jesus' life, death, and resurrection in terms that would suggest one was no more important than the other.

For me, the work of Walter Wink was essential to helping me articulate my position on this issue. His claim is that *violence never redeems*, but rather it is love that is redemptive. Now, some will argue that the sacrifice made by God and Jesus is the ultimate expression of love. Personally, I don't see much love in such a violent act.

Did God send Jesus to humanity? I believe so. Did we kill him? I believe we did. As such, it's my understanding that Jesus died *because of our sinfulness*, and because his message of radical love and justice posed such a threat to established power systems. His life embodied the notion of the end of justifiable violence. The way he lived and the way he died point the way for how humanity may find redemption from such darkness and violence.

I tend to believe that God cannot create any creature whose evil God cannot also bear and forgive. The idea of redemptive sacrifice is ancient, but I do not believe it is Christian.

Hugh Hollowell

In theological terms, you are asking about atonement theory, or, put simply, what did the death of Jesus mean or accomplish, if anything.

Believing that Jesus died for our sins, and thus somehow placated God, is a popular view of what the death of Jesus accomplished, but it is far from the only one.

Other popular views include the Christus Victor view (that by his death, Jesus overcame the work of the devil), the ransom view (that the death of Jesus somehow ransomed us from the devil) and my personal favorite, the moral example view (which says that Jesus was our example, and if you live a life like his, the powers that be will try to kill you, too).

So no, not everyone believes that the death of Jesus was all about his "dying for our sins." But that does not mean they aren't a Christian, or that the death of Jesus does not figure heavily in their faith.

Two Friars and a Fool

In brief, no. Almost all Christians believe that Jesus' death was important, but even the Christians who say "Jesus died for our sins" mean different things. Looking into the past, there have been *at least* five big answers to the question of what Jesus' crucifixion meant:

1. God defeats Satan and Death by tricking them into killing Jesus, who then breaks out of hell, ending their dominion.
2. Jesus pays our cosmic sacrificial debt for moral failure, thus ransoming us out of captivity to sin, and claiming us for God.
3. God, constrained by holiness, must punish sinners, so Jesus takes the punishment on our behalf.
4. Jesus is the moral example who shows us a way of self-sacrificial living that leads to freedom, which God vindicates through resurrection.
5. God secures meaning for us even in experiences of extreme suffering through the presence of Jesus on the cross.

What strikes us is how incredibly boring and banal it would be if Jesus' death only meant one thing, or even only a few specific things. A person could just learn the "one true answer," memorize it, and stop thinking about it or struggling with it.

Leaders of God's people and government officials killed Jesus! Jesus was and is God! Jesus forgave them even in his death-throes! Jesus cried out that God had abandoned him! Jesus came back after that and ate fish!

Nothing about that is simple. You look to the cross, you come face to face with mystery. That's what makes this so fun.

* * * * * *

Scriptural reference(s):

Matthew 5:38–48; John 3:16; Romans 8; Colossians 1:15–20

Suggested additional sources:

- *Jesus and Nonviolence: A Third Way* by Walter Wink
- *The Powers that Be* by Walter Wink
- *Love, Violence, and the Cross* by Gregory Anderson Love
- *Crucified God* by Jürgen Moltmann

- *Christus Victor: An Historical Study of the Three Main Types of the Idea of Atonement* by Gustav Aulén (trans. A. G. Hebert, SSM)

Questions for further discussion/thought:

1. Do you believe there can be salvation from sin without Jesus' blood being shed? Why or why not?

2. How do we reconcile this idea of God sending his Son to be sacrificed with the idea of an all-loving, all-merciful God?

3. Consider a famous movie, poem, or painting. Can it be reduced to a single interpretation or meaning, or does it have enough depth to support various readings?

4. Have you ever encountered an explanation of Jesus' crucifixion—and why it is important—which left unanswered questions, or didn't satisfy? What was the explanation, and why wasn't it satisfactory?

5. Looking above at five major things that Christians throughout history have said about the importance and meaning of Jesus' death on the cross, do you have a favorite? Is there one or more you've never heard before?

Source cited:

- *Jesus and Nonviolence: A Third Way* by Walter Wink (Minneapolis: Fortress, 2003)

Contributors to *You Can't Ask That*

Brian Ammons is an educator, spiritual director, author, and ordained Baptist minister. (137, 146, 155, 159)

Joan Ball is a marketing professor at St. John's University in New York. (118, 123, 127)

Nadia Bolz-Weber is an ordained Lutheran pastor, founder of House for All Sinners & Saints in Denver, Colorado, and author of three best-selling memoirs. (4, 63)

Jason Boyett is the author of several books about faith, history, and culture, including *The Pocket Guide to the Apocalypse* and *The Pocket Guide to the Afterlife*. (3, 17, 33, 41, 48, 55)

Jonathan Brooks is a speaker, writer, artist, community activist, and senior pastor of Canaan Community Church in Chicago. (141, 144, 150, 176, 196)

Lee C. Camp is a professor at Lipscomb University in Nashville and hosts "Tokens: The Podcast." (74, 124)

Bart Campolo is a former pastor and is an American humanist speaker and writer. (178, 181, 202)

Adam J. Copeland is an author, former pastor, and professor at Luther Seminary. (159, 184, 187, 189)

Craig Detweiler is a writer, filmmaker, cultural commentator, and the president of Wedgewood Circle. (3, 10, 42)

R. M. Keelan Downton is a former philosophy and religion instructor. (81, 113, 121, 124, 128, 132)

Joshua Einsohn is a casting director for a number of successful television shows. He was an activist for marriage equality in California. (16, 21, 33, 46, 64)

Sherri Emmons is an author and editor in Indianapolis. (85, 97, 105, 112, 127)

Kathy Escobar co-pastors at The Refuge, a Christian community and mission center in North Denver and is the author of *Practicing: Changing Yourself to Change the World* and several other books. (15, 26, 31, 45, 70)

Marcia Ford is an editor, journalist, and author who lives in the Rockies. (11, 23, 50, 69)

Tripp Fuller is the founder and co-host of "Homebrewed Christianity" podcast and coauthor of *Transforming Christian Theology*. (121, 130)

Becky Garrison is an American religious satirist and author. She is a 2013 recipient of a Knight Grant for Reporting on Religion and American Public Life. (6, 9, 29, 50, 58, 88, 111, 113)

Brandon Gilvin is pastor of First Christian Church (Disciples of Christ) in Chattanooga, Tennessee. (37, 51, 107, 117)

Sean Gladding is a storyteller, pastor, community gardener, backyard chicken keeper, and youth soccer coach. (170, 191, 196)

Chris Haw is an author, speaker, and theology professor at the University of Scranton. (73, 80, 83, 104, 114, 120, 133)

Hugh Hollowell is a writer, a farmer, a pastor, and a foster parent who loves cats. (148, 154, 160, 178, 184, 203)

Phil Jackson serves youth and young adults in Chicago's North Lawndale community. (142, 156, 163, 187, 194, 197)

Pablo A. Jiménez is the associate dean of the Hispanic Ministries Program at Gordon-Conwell Theological Seminary. (76, 99)

David J. Lose is the senior pastor of Mount Olivet Lutheran Church in Minneapolis and formerly the president of the Lutheran Theological Seminary at Philadelphia. (40, 48, 54, 58, 66, 103, 125)

Andrew Marin is founder and current president of the Marin Foundation. (137, 153, 155, 172, 175, 193)

Jarrod McKenna is the cofounder of First Home Project, a community for welcoming and housing refugees. (13, 29, 37, 66, 74, 80, 92, 105, 120, 123)

Carol Howard Merritt   is an author, seminary instructor, and congregational pastor in Connecticut. (162, 165, 169)

L. Shannon Moore is the senior associate minister at University Christian Church (Disciples of Christ) in Fort Worth, Texas. (88, 93, 101, 114, 134)

José F. Morales Jr. is a professor at Chicago Theological Seminary in Illinois. (4, 18, 22, 25, 34, 60, 100)

Doug Pagitt is an author, pastor, social activist, and executive director and cofounder of Vote Common Good. (144, 182, 200)

Gary Peluso-Verdend is the former president of Phillips Theological Seminary in Tulsa, Oklahoma. (21, 25, 38, 41, 44, 60, 64, 69)

Christian Piatt is an author, editor, speaker, musician, and spoken-word artist whose books include the original *Banned Questions* series, the *Surviving the Bible* series, and *Post-Christian*. (5, 15, 75, 117, 166, 203)

Jim L. Robinson is pastor of First Christian Church (Disciples of Christ) in Conway, Arkansas. (6, 13, 27, 33, 52, 56, 67)

Phil Shepherd, a.k.a. the Whiskey Preacher, lived and pastored congregations across North America. (156, 193)

Phil Snider is pastor of Brentwood Christian Church (Disciples of Christ) in Springfield, Missouri. (83, 99, 103, 108, 129, 150, 169, 180, 185, 190, 199)

Margot Starbuck is an author, speaker, editor, and literary collaborator. (138, 141, 146, 148, 160, 175)

Mark Van Steenwyk is the executive director of the Center for Prophetic Imagination in Minneapolis, Minnesota. (89, 93, 107, 111)

Joshua Toulouse is pastor of The Table, a congregation in Knoxville, Tennessee. (5, 18, 23, 27, 35, 59)

Matthew Paul Turner is a blogger, speaker, and author of sixteen books, including the best-selling *When God Made You* and *When God Made Light*. (153, 162, 173, 180, 189, 199)

Two Friars and a Fool is actually three people: Nick Larson is a dad, digital consultant, and minister in Columbia, Missouri; Aric Clark is an activist and a pastor in Portland, Oregon; and Doug Hagler is a pastor, writer, and gamer in the Phoenixville, Pennsylvania, area. (139, 151, 166, 179, 204)

Peter J. Walker is focused on men's work and exploring healthy masculinity, primarily through the Mankind Project. (84, 91, 97, 108, 134)

Rebecca Bowman Woods is an editor and spiritual care coordinator at a mental health facility in Ohio. (9, 30, 44, 54, 71)

Amy Reeder Worley is lawyer, management consultant, writer, Presbyterian, and mother based in Raleigh, North Carolina. (76, 79, 85, 91, 96, 115, 129, 132)